MANON:
ALONE IN FRONT OF THE NET

MANON RHÉAUME
with
CHANTAL GILBERT

HarperCollins*PublishersLtd*

Translated by Mark Daly

Photographs courtesy of Nicole Rhéaume,
unless otherwise indicated.

First Edition

Canadian Cataloguing in Publication Data

Rhéaume, Manon
Manon : alone in front of the net

ISBN 0-00-638029-8

1. Rhéaume, Manon.
2. Hockey players — Canada — Biography.
3. Women athletes — Canada — Biography.
I. Gilbert, Chantal.
II. Title.

GV848.5.R44A3 1993   796.962'092   C93-093509-8

93 94 95 96 97 98 99 ❖ EB 10 9 8 7 6 5 4 3 2 1

MANON:
ALONE IN FRONT OF THE NET

60 YEARS IN CANADA

19 33
19 93

HarperCollins

CONTENTS

FOREWORD

This is no fairy tale. This is a story about a simple life, a life full of all the great joys and profound sadnesses felt by virtually every one of us. Moments of exhilaration and triumph; moments of pit-of-the-stomach anguish.

I love this life and I savor every minute of it because I know what I went through to get where I am.

I remember all the hurdles I had to leap, the taboos I demolished. I remember the pain and suffering I endured without shedding a tear, so no one could call me a crybaby little girl.

I am only too aware of the uproar my presence in the macho world of hockey has caused. Some of the players can't accept the fact that a woman was suddenly catapulted into the pro leagues without paying her dues at the Junior A level. And a lot of sports reporters won't even give me the time of day.

For most people, I'm nothing but a publicity stunt.

No, this life is no illusion. It's a dream—my dream. And my dream is, almost unbelievably, coming true.

I won't deny it: I was in the right place at the right time, with the right people in my corner. Born under the right sign, perhaps. But tell me truthfully: if you were given an opportunity to reach for the stars, would you walk away? Would you refuse the chance to live out your wildest fantasies? Would you walk away from your greatest desires?

Would you be afraid to try?

And would you deny a person barely twenty years of age the chance to excel?

Surely not!

Well, I was offered a chance to live out my dream. How could I pass it up? If I had, I knew that someday I would have to look back and ask myself: "What might have happened if I had accepted Phil Esposito's offer? Where would I be now? How far might I have gone?" If I had declined his offer, I wouldn't have been able to face myself in the mirror. I'd have died of shame.

My life is very intense, full of magical moments. A real jet-set existence: limousines, fan mail, autograph-signing sessions, sumptuous banquets, meeting political, sports and entertainment personalities. It kind of takes your breath away! But it isn't all peaches and cream. It's also very demanding and tiring, even now that I'm twenty-one. The practices, the packed schedules, the media and their often excessively harsh criticism. It's tough ... sometimes too tough. But mainly, it's the loneliness that's hard to deal with. In Atlanta, far from my home for the first time in my life, I feel very alone. It's a big city where I don't know a soul, and it scares me a bit.

Being the first woman to play in professional hockey is no big deal to me. Ever since I was a little girl, I have been "the first" to do lots of things. Nothing new there. What matters to me is constantly outdoing myself.

So that's what I'm doing ... I'm going as far as I can.

Sometimes, I have to admit, it all does sound a bit like a fairy tale come true!

MANON:
ALONE IN FRONT OF THE NET

1

THE IMPOSSIBLE DREAM

I've always been crazy about hockey, and the idea of playing professionally has been the impossible dream that replays in my head, endlessly.

Who would have believed me if I had said, at the age of five: "When I grow up, I'm going to be a goalie in the big leagues"? Everyone would have laughed at the silly idea, for sure.

Happily, my parents believed in me and kept an open mind. Not that they didn't need a little encouragement—I had to do a bit of convincing! But generally I get what I go after in life, and that's been the case since I was a little girl.

I grew up in Lac Beauport, a city in the mountains a few kilometers north of Quebec City. My father, Pierre, married young and fell in love with this part of the province while horseback riding. He boarded his horse, Aramis, with a local farmer, and whenever he had even a few minutes, he mounted his faithful friend and sought refuge from the city in the quiet woods and fields. In this way, he was able to escape his downtown construction business: no more plans, excavations, late deliveries of material, workers who called in sick on the hottest days. No more stink of hot tar or splinters in his fingers. His business monopolized his time; it was only on his flights to the country that he could relax and gather his thoughts.

The idea of moving his family to Lac Beauport came to him just prior to the birth of my older brother, Martin. My mother, Nicole, didn't object. An athletic woman herself, she liked the idea of the nearby mountains and lake and looked forward to downhill skiing and swimming.

My dad built our first house with his own hands. It was pretty and comfortable, but we soon outgrew it. Martin was not yet two when I arrived on February 24, 1972, and my brother Pascal followed soon after.

So we needed a larger house. A bit of a visionary, Dad built it for a family of athletes. Anyone who walked in would immediately notice the line of hooks on the wall for dozens of ski jackets and snowsuits, and the heaps of hockey skates, sticks and skis. The basement belonged to the kids, and we continued our hockey games down there. The walls still bear the battle scars!

My father, a persistent and brave man, got me involved in hockey, instilling in me his desire to reach for the stars. He taught me about pride and dignity, equality and respect.

A sports fan in general and a hockey fan in particular, he had always helped organize community sports. Martin was not even old enough to play hockey when my dad decided it would be a good idea to make a backyard skating rink for the local kids. He couldn't understand how an outdoors-oriented place like Lac Beauport, in a part of the country where snow and cold are the masters, could lack a proper hockey rink. He couldn't accept that his son wouldn't be able to play hockey in his hometown when he got older.

The mayor of Lac Beauport was certainly keen for my father to build the rink, but after that, he was on his own! In the mayor's opinion, Lac Beauport was a ski center, period. After a lot of negotiation, the mayor agreed that the town would pay for the boards and other necessities, on the condition that the residents build and maintain the rink. My father rallied his friends and neighbors and everyone pledged to do their bit to help.

The mayor gave them a piece of land that was not exactly a developer's dream: there was a one-foot variation in the level of the ground from one side of the property to the other. But they believed in what they were trying to achieve and they pulled it off! The hours they spent at night flooding it ... what drudgery! But what a rink!

Even though Martin couldn't really use the rink yet, it gave my dad immense pleasure to watch the local kids skating. He coached them in skating techniques, showing them how to skate forward, backward, turn, cut across. If the skating session had gone well, then he might allow the puck on the ice during the last fifteen minutes. Only then would he let the kids try passing and shooting.

My father shares the Russian hockey philosophy: there's no big hurry to get the puck out on the ice. North American parents generally disagree. They want to see their kids pushing a puck around as soon as possible so they can get it into the net. But five- and six-year-old children are too young for that pressure.

As part of his coaching role, my father borrowed a sound system and sweaters from his hometown of Saint-Albert-le-Grand in Quebec City's Lower Town area. Every week, he dragged his little team's equipment back and forth in his own car.

Thanks to my father, Lac Beauport's hockey team thrived. Even though most of the kids were dedicated skiers as well—among my father's protégés were the Laroche brothers, the world-renowned freestyle skiers—they took their hockey training seriously, and it started to show.

I began skating at a very tender age, when I was barely three. I was so proud of my little skates. They were white figure skates, the kind all girls wore in those days. At the time, my parents could never had imagined—nor could I—that someday I would need boys' skates.

When Martin started playing hockey at about the age of seven, Pascal wanted to imitate his big brother. At four years old he was still a bit young, but he raised such a storm of protest that Dad had to allow him on the team. And anyway, it was his team, right? Since the original idea was to get as many kids on the ice as possible, why not Pascal?

Since we three siblings were always together, I played in all my brothers' games. In the street, in the backyard, in the basement, summer and winter, we played hockey together. I was their goaltender while they practiced their shots and passes. The fact of the matter was that I was more a live obstacle in front of the net, or the third goalpost. I was keen, but like most five-year-olds, this didn't necessarily translate into skill or reflexes. But I spent hours trying to stop their shots and I never grew tired of it.

Stimulated by the presence of his own two boys on his team, my dad became more and more involved in organizing local hockey. With his friends from neighboring towns he created the Northern League. Friendly, but well-organized just the same, its main objective was to allow local kids to play and have fun.

Practices were now held every Sunday at the arena in Charlesbourg, a neighboring community. While the two boys sweated it out on the rink and Dad coached, my mother and I sat in the stands watching and cheering—the traditional family scene. But it was written in the stars that the picture would change. And rather quickly, at that.

It wasn't in my nature to sit watching passively. Family togetherness is nice, but sitting for hours in the stands watching my two brothers play ... no thanks! I had to move. Day after day I sat and fidgeted as my passion to play hockey grew. And grew. Slowly. Quietly.

I wanted to be in the net, blocking that puck. That was my idea of heaven. That's when I began to dream my impossible dream: to play hockey, real hockey, and to climb higher and higher, until I made it to the big leagues. Not a night went by that I didn't dream this dream.

Because my father's vision of learning hockey skills involved all practice and no games, there was no goalie on my dad's team, just regular players. But the day inevitably came when he had to enter his team in a Northern League tournament. Only then did it dawn upon him that he had no netminder.

He was at a bit of a loss, because none of his players had a clue how to be a goalie. Besides, he didn't want to penalize any of his little protégés, all of whom wanted to play up front. He wanted them all to play in a real game, to have a chance to practice the skating maneuvers and hockey strategies he had taught them. He knew that the player he chose to guard the goal would take it as a punishment of some kind, a "demotion." He was really upset. What to do?

In my mind's eye, I can still see the family around the dinner table, Mom and Dad discussing the problem, and five-year-old me, picking away at my plate, playing with bits of salad and spinning my milk glass like a top, antsy as anything, squirming away in my chair, wanting to speak. And finally, unable to hold the words back any longer, spitting it out: "Why not me? I come every Sunday to watch Martin and Pascal play, but I never get to play! I sit in the stands. I just get to watch. And I know all the other guys, too! And I play goalie all the time with Martin and Pascal when we play in the backyard and the basement. I could do it, Daddy! Please? Let me be your goalie. Please, please, please, Daddy?"

Poor guy! I had him right where I wanted him.

"Well, okay, why not, eh, little girl?"

You should have seen my mother's face! She couldn't have been more shocked if I'd asked for a tarantula for Christmas.

Think about it. There weren't too many parents back in 1977 who would have allowed their little girl to "dress up" like a boy. Even today, there isn't exactly wide acceptance of the idea of girls playing hockey. My mother would have preferred that I take up another sport, like figure skating or gymnastics, or simply devote myself to downhill skiing, which I was already good at and which I could practice practically right next door.

"Hockey! That's for the boys, not for you," she tried to say.

But my father finally brought her over to my side, and she eventually agreed: "Why not? She seems to love being in net. Why stop her? I wouldn't want anyone to prevent me from playing a sport, no matter what it was."

Finally, with my mother's blessing, my goaltending career could start in earnest.

Finally, I could begin to really kindle my passion.

Finally, my impossible dream was becoming possible.

Sunday, the day of the big game, finally came. The morning seemed interminable. I couldn't sit still for five minutes.

Suddenly, it was time to get ready. As usual, my brothers got ahead of the game by putting on some of their equipment at home. I did the same. God, I was excited!

I was barely in the door of the arena when my parents insisted that I don my goaltender's mask. I guess they didn't want everyone to know I was a girl too soon. They didn't want to have to deal with the remarks. And they wanted me to be judged on my performance, not on the fact that I was a girl.

Right from the start, I had something to prove. I was already being looked at askance because I was a little girl who liked playing hockey with her brothers and their friends. That was all right in the backyard and basement, perhaps, but in arenas ...?

I was really going against local custom in Quebec, where hockey is almost a religion: in this province, hockey is definitely a boys' sport. Girls play ringette. ("There's no way that little brat's going to steal *my* boy's place on the team ... he's going all the way to the National Hockey League!")

In Quebec, even at the very lowest levels, hockey is extremely competitive. Parents get really caught up in their boys' performances. They scream from the stands. They try to influence coaches, managers and scouts. Many parents take a loss by their child's team very hard. They give everybody hell, their children included. I can't even imagine how many kids have abandoned hockey entirely because they were fed up with their parents' lectures. When you're young, you want to play for fun, and that's the way it should be.

My parents understood that. They always took a positive approach with us. Their criticism was constructive and we learned from our mistakes. They never put us down.

This first hockey game at the arena was very funny. The boys on my team were not too surprised to see me. They all recognized me, and at that age, kids are not too prejudiced.

We were all very excited to be playing our first hockey game, but you could hardly have called it the game of the century. My own performance in goal was unremarkable—about what you'd expect from a five-year-old child, being tripped up by her leg pads, awkward with her huge gloves, and having trouble keeping her balance on her skates.

I always wore my white figure skates. This was the only detail that gave away my femininity. After the game, I asked my father to file the big teeth off the tip of my skate blades so I wouldn't trip. My mind was already made up: figure skating wasn't for me. I would play hockey, and I would be a goaltender.

At that point, I was totally unaware of the adventure into which I was throwing myself—an experience full of pitfalls, politics, battles and concessions. But I've never had to act in any way against my free will or conscience. I have always guarded my self-respect in my decisions and actions and, most of the time, I've won the respect of those around me.

NICOLE RHÉAUME

Martin was two when Manon was born on February 24, 1972. She decided to come into this world between two ferocious snowstorms. The snowplows were having difficulty clearing the streets. They had to pass by with a snowblower first. It was like nothing we'd ever seen.

The labor was long and difficult, but what a beautiful baby we had! Not difficult or whiny. I used to wrap her up well in her carriage and let her sleep outside. Manon was our lovely, rosy-cheeked ice fairy.

Fifteen months later, Pascal came along. The arrival of a new little brother made Manon a bit wild. Strangers couldn't come close to her or even look at her sideways. She would make such a fuss if anyone tried to talk to her or smile at her. Even Pierre couldn't handle her himself when I had to leave the house. I was the only one she wanted.

The children started skating young. Manon had her first skates when she was three. She learned the basics of skating pretty quickly. She didn't want anyone to hold her hand.

When this little girl learned something, she learned fast. She didn't have to be shown twice. She'd be there, watching with her piercing little eyes, saying, "Let me do it! Get out of my way!" It was the same for everything. She's still like that. She's a quick learner.

Even as a tot, she was a real snoop. In her efforts to see everything, she'd do acrobatics that would make me tremble.

Twice we had to take her to the hospital. The first time, it was a broken arm at two years old. The second time, at age three, it was for a concussion. She had fallen off Pierre's workbench. I couldn't leave her alone for two minutes.

I wouldn't say she was a daredevil, just a go-getter. She wanted to do everything herself, without asking anyone for help, so she often took risks.

While Martin and Pascal were daredevils and never hurt themselves, Manon was always breaking something. The boys did crazy things on skis all day and came home safe and sound. She would practice her style in powder snow, being very careful, and break a leg.

She wasn't lucky. She always had something in a cast.

I can still see her in our backyard skating rink, one leg in a cast up to the hip. She couldn't play with her team, but that wasn't going to stop her from playing goal with her brothers.

If she was hard on herself, it was probably because of us. I would hear her little cries of pain sometimes and it pulled at my heartstrings. But I trusted Pierre. He was hard with her sometimes, but he never would have let her try things she couldn't do. He wouldn't tolerate danger.

Interestingly, as much as she was a go-getter and brave in front of the puck, she was often a very fearful child in everyday life.

When Pierre and I would go out for an evening, she would be beside herself with worry. Most times she would get herself invited to Mireille's, Pierre's sister. If she couldn't arrange that, she would go to bed earlier than her brothers so that she would be asleep and oblivious to the normal nighttime creaking and groaning of our big house.

If she was unlucky enough to wake up in the night and realize that we weren't home, she'd climb into bed with Pascal or Martin to get back to sleep.

She still is a bit afraid. Maybe it's because I always watched the TV news. She wasn't interested in the picture, but she heard what was being said all the same. She'd hear them talking about robberies and kidnappings and rapes and murders. Maybe she was affected by all these stories.

Even now, she doesn't like to stay alone in the house, go out alone at night or drive in strange neighborhoods.

2

HEY GUYS, I'M HERE!

My early career as goaltender was a series of small battles. I was always the first girl, the one who opened the door. I had to prove that I deserved my place. I had to deal with everyone's doubts all the time.

At five years old, in my first real game, I had no doubt that this would be my lot for my whole life.

My first pre-novice season was not very long, but it was very funny. I learned the basics of my sport on the job. I had no technique and only the rudimentary reflexes of a five-year-old. My skating skills were limited, but I was a keener. I already saw myself at the Quebec City International Peewee Hockey Tournament, the annual event to which all young Quebec hockey players aspire.

My parents had a good laugh when they heard this. They thought I was dreaming in technicolor, that I'd forget this idea at the end of the season and take up skiing or figure skating. The following year, however, right at the beginning of the season, I registered officially as a goalie for my father's team.

I shared goaltending duties with a friend, Guy Duchesne. He was a little older than I was. At six years old, I was too young to be goalie when our team entered an Atom tournament. At those times, I played defense and he played in net.

I remember one tournament when I played two games in a row, the first as a goalie in the novice category, and immediately after on defense for the Atoms. I had to perform some real gymnastics to change uniform at the edge of the rink between games!

More than one person is concerned about the issue of gender and athletes' locker rooms. It is an intriguing question.

In the beginning, it wasn't a problem for me. All the children arrived at the arena with their uniforms already on and went back home to change. It was just easier for the parents. We were so small, we couldn't put our uniforms on by ourselves anyway. Later, I would put on my jogging pants and my black, long-sleeved sweater and would join the boys in the locker room when they already had their uniforms on. While I finished dressing, the coach would give his instructions.

After the game, I was always the first one in the locker room, alone for a few minutes, enough time to take off my wet clothes, dry myself with a towel and put something fresh on. I would shower at home. Sometimes there was a small room for me at the arena but that was strictly a luxury.

Those who are concerned about this issue should be reassured: nothing traumatic ever happened in the locker rooms, either for myself or the boys. There was plenty of privacy and mutual respect.

*   *   *

By the time I reached Atom age, eight years old, the Northern League was well organized and going full blast. There were good tournaments, and I had to give up my goalie position to another teammate. It was clear that he was better than I was. I was heartbroken not to be tending goal, but those were the rules of the game. It was fair.

Since leaving hockey was out of the question, I played defense. In the end, this was a good thing for me. I improved my backwards skating technique. I learned to hold my stick better, to carry the puck and to check. This gave me a different perspective on the game. I learned a lot that was very useful later on.

The next year, the other goalie advanced to Peewee, leaving the goalie position open. I regained my position, but in the meantime I had learned a valuable lesson: I had to improve my technique if I wanted to hang on to my spot. So I asked my parents to sign me up for goaltending school during the summer. They sent my brothers to similar camps, so why not me? They readily agreed.

I remember going to the registration table ... I can laugh about it now, but at the time, I didn't find it funny. Two men were there to greet the children.

"What's your name?"

"Manon Rhéaume."

"Pardon me, I didn't get that."

"Manon Rhéaume."

"I think you've made a mistake. The ringette camp is next door."

"My name is Manon and I'm here for the hockey goaltending school."

"Eh!?"

"Yes! Goaltending!"

"What the heck is this!? Well, okay. Go ahead. We'll soon see."

Never will I forget the sidelong glances, the dry, mocking tone of those men.

But already at eight years of age, it took more than that to discourage me. I took my hockey bag and, after glancing back at my parents, I joined the other kids.

At camp I was a bit of a sneak: when the coach explained a new technique that we had to try, I would always let three or four other goalies go ahead of me. The coach would correct them and I would listen to his advice. When it was my turn, I'd try the technique with the coach's comments in mind.

This paid off. The coach thought I was talented and paid a lot of attention to me. I learned a lot and left really pumped up—"Bring on those pucks!"

I returned to my team with improved techniques and sharper reflexes. I was more flexible, faster, had better balance. I was solid, ready for a new season. Let's just say I was really starting to look like a goalie.

The 1980-81 season went well. Like all other teams, we won about as many as we lost. But the scores were always close.

Then one day Christian Beaudouin, my father's coaching assistant, suggested trying Benoît-Luc Nolin in nets. He had seen Benoît-Luc playing ball hockey on the street, stopping the balls with spectacular moves, making kamikaze leaps and last-second catches in his glove with his arm stretched to the limit. He seemed very impressed with Benoît-Luc's skills.

I knew Benoît-Luc well. We competed together on the ski hills and played hockey on the same team. He was a very good hockey player, true, but he had never played in net during a real game. I liked him a lot, but to share my goaltending duties with him—now, that was asking too much.

It was my father who came to warn me:

"Manon, you won't be the goalie in tomorrow's game."

"What's going on? Why are you telling me this? Why wouldn't I be in net? I won my position fair and square and I'm keeping it."

"Manon, when you calm down, you'll understand. Mr. Beaudouin wants to try Benoît-Luc. He saw him playing in the street near his house and thought he was amazing."

"What? Benoît-Luc Nolin? But playing on ice isn't the same as playing on the street. Boots and skates ... you know what I'm talking about, Daddy!"

"Calm down. I'm not sure that Benoît-Luc can do it. But you'll play defense in the next game and we'll see what happens. Let him play and we'll have a clear conscience. Everyone will know that you deserve your position and that Benoît-Luc doesn't have what it takes to be a goalie. But if you leave any doubt in the minds of Benoît-Luc and Christian Beaudouin, it will spread to the locker room, to the entire league. The ball will start rolling. People will start to wonder and it won't stop. They'll say that I'm protecting you and your position. I want peace. It's important for me, but more for you. We have to remove the doubt. If not, we'll have to live with it for a long time."

With a heavy heart I agreed to play defense, but I understood.

17

I understood that I had to fight the doubts, the precon-
ceived ideas, the old mentality. I was the first girl to take a
chance in this men's world of hockey. At only eight years old,
I was entering my first battle.

So the next day, Benoît-Luc took his place between the
posts at the Saint-Augustin arena, and I played defense.

Poor Benoît-Luc! It must have been awful for him. Very
quickly, our team was down 4-0. Making spectacular stops on
a paved road, wearing boots, is not the same as on a slippery
surface, wearing skates. God, those pucks were flying into the
net from all directions.

I liked Benoît-Luc a lot and I wished him no ill; I even felt
sorry for him. But I couldn't help smiling. In the second
period, I could hear the comments of my teammates: "What's
with this decision? It doesn't make any sense. Why doesn't
the coach put Manon back in? We're going to lose."

We didn't just lose, we were steamrollered 9-1. Our team
lost, but I won something. The doubt dissolved like smoke.
The other players wanted me back in net. I really felt that I was
their goalie, that I had their confidence and that they respected
me. And I had the satisfaction of having won my first battle.

Life had taught me an important lesson: it's not by avoid-
ing a problem, but by facing it, that you solve it. I learned this
lesson at a young age. It served me well and still does. Whenever I have the opportunity, I try to share it with the young
children I meet.

In my last Atom year, 1983, the town of Lac Beauport signed an
agreement. We would now be playing hockey in cooperation

with the neighboring city, Charlesbourg. This big Quebec City suburb had arenas and a large hockey organization. I had to enter a new environment where no one knew me, and where no one was used to seeing a girl on hockey skates. Once again, I was going to have to prove myself!

I arrived at the Atom AA training camp with my younger brother, Pascal. Everything went smoothly for both of us. We started with eight goalies, and I made it to the final cut, with three goalies left. I gave it my best shot, but in the end I was cut anyway. I ended up in the category just below, Atom CC.

Was it perhaps because I was a girl and the men were not used to seeing a girl play in net? I was a pioneer, and maybe they weren't ready to accept this new phenomenon. I'll never know. So once again I had to prove myself, this time in Charlesbourg, and crush the doubts.

"Let's get it over with! Bring on the games and the pucks. I'll show you what I can do."

I didn't have to wait long to show them!

The first time I was able to prove my talent was during a round-robin tournament in Asbestos, Quebec. It started badly. Our first game was against the Asbestos team, the previous year's grand champions, and we lost 6-1. But after this initial defeat, things began to look up, and we won all the other regular games.

Finally, we found ourselves again facing Asbestos in the championship final. The day before the big game, reporters conducted interviews. They were touting the game as a major battle. The arena was full. The atmosphere was incredible. Within two minutes, our team had scored the first goal. From that point on, the game became a series of end-to-end attacks—a real tennis match.

In the beginning, the Asbestos fans were 100 percent behind their team, which was only natural. But by the third period, I could sense a change of heart. They cheered when one of their players attacked, but they also clapped enthusiastically when I made the save. What a feeling! This was true sportsmanship, the spirit that any real fan should have. There was none of the violence, the nastiness that so often pervades the stands.

The game finally ended 1-0. We had dethroned the champions, and I was voted most valuable player of the game.

The next day, I made page one of the newspapers: "The Ace of Aces Beats Asbestos!" This was my first taste of glory and my first experience with the media.

I will always have fond memories of the Asbestos tournament. Everyone was so nice, and I didn't feel any animosity, any hatred from the public. The competition was restricted to the ice, between children, the way it should be, with the greatest respect for the opponent.

In addition, my strong performance showed the people in the Charlesbourg organization what I was made of. I was not a boy, granted, but that didn't stop me from having guts and character.

I wanted to show them that I wasn't scared of the puck and that I could take as much as the boys. I had become accustomed at a very young age to enduring pain without crying, because I didn't want people to say things like, "Of course she's crying! She's a girl. She's too soft to be a goalie, get her out of there!" I could leave the rink at the end of the game covered in bruises without anyone knowing. I didn't grimace in pain or rub my wounds. I blinked back my tears. The only time I didn't get up from the ice right away was when I suffered a concussion after colliding with one of my defensemen. I woke up in the hospital.

It's because of a stinging remark that my father once made to me that I am always able to get back on my feet: "Manon, macramé isn't painful. Choose!" I choke back my tears and return to the crease.

Dad's comment has stayed with me and still gives me strength in difficult times. I recalled it recently, during a game with the Trois-Rivières Draveurs of the Quebec Major Junior Hockey League, when I was taking advantage of a time-out to rub my eye because I was seeing everything in a fog, as if through a yellow filter. My eyebrow had just been cut by my mask, which had been broken by a hard shot. My face was all bloody. But never would I have fallen down, or asked the referee to stop the game.

I don't want to take dives, as so many goalies do. I can't. I have to remain on my feet. I endure my pain, say nothing and continue to do my job: tending goal.

PIERRE RHÉAUME

This little girl created her own luck. She set her own goal and achieved it. It's almost as though she could predict the future.

Even as a small child, Manon had her mind set on playing hockey with her brothers. She ended up in net because her brothers wanted to practice their shots. She wanted to be worthy of her brothers, so she worked hard. That's always been her approach.

Her dream was to play hockey. Her battle was to have people let her improve and develop, just like the other players.

When she first told us she wanted to play, we thought it was cute. Nicole and I thought it was just a phase. A season or two and she'd forget about it. She'd end up in figure skating, like all the other bright little girls. But no!

Hockey became her passion. All we wanted was for her to be happy.

Manon has an unusually strong character and an enormous sense of pride. When she decides on something, it has to happen. Even as a little girl she announced that she would play in the Quebec City International Peewee Hockey Tournament. That was her goal. Nicole and I laughed. But the future was to prove her right. She played in the tournament—not just once, but three times.

Still, we thought this idea would pass quickly. But, when she started asking us to register her in hockey schools, like her brothers, we started taking her seriously.

In her last Peewee year, at thirteen, she was still saying: "Next year, I'm going to try for the Bantam AA camp and I'll make it. I won't be cut. I'm going to play Bantam AA, for sure." She worked so hard that she succeeded.

To get where she is, Manon had to work very hard.

She didn't complain often about the tough hits she received. I remember one time when she was still little that she came to me with tears in her eyes and told me that she had been hurt by a player's shot. That was when I told her that macramé isn't painful. If looks could kill, I would have been dead before she headed back out onto the ice.

It was a tough thing to say, but if I'd reacted to her tears, she would have become used to complaining. Then her critics would have said: "See. You can't have a girl on a team. You have to look after her and baby her."

I had to make her become tougher than a boy, because when she'd take a puck in her mask and fall on her back, you'd could hear the shouts from the crowd: "Naturally. She's just a girl." Whenever the same thing happened to a boy, you'd hear instead: "Did you see that shot? Great stop!"

Poor Manon became so good at not complaining that it got to the point of being almost dangerous. She developed quite a high level of tolerance.

Even when she was little, when she'd break a wrist or a leg skiing, get a sprain or rip the skin off her tongue on a frozen pole at an outdoor rink, Manon reacted like a grown-up. It was really surprising. Even the doctors found it unusual.

I remember one time in particular when she was playing at the Peewee level. She'd broken a toe when she banged into a piece of furniture at the house. She absolutely refused to miss a week of hockey so it would heal. So I had to tie the broken toe to another, and she played the games as though nothing had happened. Not a grimace, not a whimper.

One day she came to me and said, "This is crazy. My thigh is black." She showed me her leg. The inside of her thigh was black from her groin to her knee. Her gear wasn't providing enough protection from the shots. Thirteen-year-olds are strong and can put a lot of power behind the puck.

I took her out right away to buy new hockey pants. She needed a new chest-protector, too. What was available didn't provide enough protection at the armpits and elbows. She was growing into a big girl with a bust and the manufacturers hadn't figured on that. I had to rely on my talent as a handyman: I made her a customized one using some fiberglass and an old pair of leg pads. It was homemade but it was still working in 1992. She wore it at the start of the season with the Atlanta Knights in November 1992.

Another time, I recall she was still in Peewee and I hurt her by accident. I had just parked at the Charlesbourg arena. She and I were taking the equipment bags and sticks out of the trunk. I closed the lid too quickly and caught her fingers.

I thought my heart would stop. It seemed like it took forever to find my keys and unlock the trunk lid. She was screaming with the pain and the tears were flowing.

Her fingers had a big blue line across them. I grabbed some snow from the ground and stuffed her hand into it to keep the swelling down and reduce the pain. As soon as she was able to make some sort of intelligible sound she pointed at me accusingly with the finger of her good hand and said, "Listen. It's my turn to play tonight. There's no way you're going to replace me. Okay?"

I didn't dare say no right away, but I knew that there wasn't much chance. "Manon, let's go in and we'll see in the dressing room. Keep your hand in the snow," I suggested.

She was alone in the dressing room and didn't want anyone to help her suit up. She'd put on one piece of gear, then take a minute to stick her hand back in the ice and hold her breath. It was pitiful.

My manager, Michel Fiset, figured it made no sense to have her play, but we let Manon decide herself.

Despite the pain, she played—and pretty well, too.

Manon is so tough that she never stayed down on the ice long, even when she was seriously hurt. A strained muscle, eyebrow cut open with blood running down her face—she never stopped. The team trainer had to pull her out of the game, warning her about this sort of recklessness. Any other goalie would have stayed down on the ice to stop the play. Not her. She never wants to lie down. She toughs it out, doesn't say a word and just keeps on tending goal.

3

A FAMILY UNITED

Hockey, hockey, hockey. It seemed that outside of school, I didn't do anything else. If my brothers and I weren't on the ice, we were in the basement playing hockey. Of course I played with my dolls, and my brothers with their Lego, but after about five minutes it was stronger than us.

"Are we going to play hockey?"

Let's go! Barbie would be flung aside and I'd grab my hockey stick. Crash, bang! We'd shove aside whatever was in the middle of the basement. My brothers would attack, pass, pirouette, and I'd stop them. We'd have shooting contests against the walls.

You should have seen the mess! My father hadn't finished the basement walls, which were covered only with blue polystyrene. Our greatest kick was to shoot the puck hard enough that it would stick in the wall and stay there. The room looked like it was being demolished.

My greatest pleasure was to play "hockey training camp." In the winter, I could play on our backyard rink. In the summer, it was on roller skates on the patio or even in the basement. If my brothers weren't available, I would invent imaginary players. There were five or six of them and they would listen to me religiously and follow my orders. I gave the good players names I liked: Steve, Jean-Philippe, Simon. Those who weren't talented were called Éric, Frédéric, names I didn't like.

I would explain a series of exercises for them to do so I could make my selection, and I would encourage them. "Go, Steve!" I'd shout. Then I would become Steve, the talented one. "Go, Éric!" Then I'd pretend that I didn't know how to skate, or I'd miss the net when I shot.

I would grade my players on a notepad, and at the end I would meet them one at a time to tell them what they were doing right and wrong, what they had to improve. I always ended by saying: "You did well, but we're not taking you."

Curiously, there were never any girls in my imaginary camps. I was never conscious of it. I just never thought of including female players in my games.

I sometimes tried to recruit my little girl neighbors, without much success. I never found them good enough and it annoyed me. I became impatient. They quickly went back to their dolls. I have to admit I kind of pushed them around.

I also played at school. I would try to get my brothers to participate in the games, but I never had much luck. After about five minutes, they would find a thousand excuses to do something else. They didn't like school to begin with, so to spend extra time in the playground playing hockey ... that was asking a bit much.

School was always very important to me. I was jealous when Martin left for school and I, being too young, had to stay home. I would invent homework and lessons to be learned. I was so excited when I finally started kindergarten at Montagnac school. Finally, I could have real homework to do after school. I could do like Martin: sit with my notebooks, my textbooks, my pencils. I liked school so much that I cried when we had holidays.

I guess I was a model student, since I loved to study. I concentrated on what I was doing and learned very quickly. It was easy for me. Teachers didn't have to explain something to me twice. When I finished my class work, I asked for more. I always wanted good grades. If someone in the class got a better grade than me, I would work harder for the next exam. I would also compete against myself. If I got 90 percent in an exam, I wanted to get 95 percent the next time and, if possible, 100 percent.

In everything I did, I had a real competitive spirit. No matter what the activity, I wanted to do as well as possible.

In second grade, my marks were so high that the teacher wanted me to skip to grade four. My mother objected. She didn't want me to go too fast and have school become too difficult for me. She did the right thing.

The only subject I didn't like was geography. All those names to remember ... it bored me to death. But I made an effort nonetheless.

On the other hand, physical education was a real pleasure. When it was time for phys ed, I was the first one in the gym. I gave it everything I had, body and soul.

I remember once when, carried away with enthusiasm, I ran right into a cement wall. I misjudged the distance and I couldn't stop running in time. I saw a lot of stars, but I only suffered a bump on my head. My teacher, Jean Bédard, was more frightened than I was. He suggested that I calm down and stay alive.

At home, my brothers and I were raised fairly liberally. Of course, we had to follow certain rules, but we had great freedom to express ourselves. Quite early on, we began calling our parents by their first names most of the time. This made sense, actually, since we didn't feel like yelling "Dad" twenty times during every practice and, at any rate, all the other players called him Pierre. We figured we might as well not be different.

The five of us were always together. As soon as we could stand up on skis, our weekends were spent together on the slopes of Le Relais, the Lac Beauport ski center. You can't live in the shadow of a ski hill without being tempted by this thrilling sport. It stays cold for so much of the year in this part of the world that one has to take advantage of all the positive aspects of winter.

Our poor parents! They encouraged us in sports to the point that we became fanatics. Saturday mornings on the ski slopes; afternoons in the arenas. Sunday, the other way around. Sometimes we would have a hockey tournament in the morning and a ski race in the afternoon. On those occasions, our parents couldn't stop looking at their watches, hoping the hockey game would end as quickly as possible. Our clothing changes were accomplished like actors backstage in the theater, on the run in the halls ... a sandwich and a juice gulped down quickly ... into the car and off to the ski hill.

Eventually, our parents started to feel like taxi drivers. They had more than enough energy and they wanted to help, but since money doesn't grow on trees and there are only twenty-four hours in a day, eventually they demanded that we choose between hockey and skiing.

My brothers and I were never forced to do something we didn't like. As long as we were having fun, that was okay. There was only one rule: we had to finish what we started. Whether it was karate, ballet, skiing, tennis or hockey, we had to think before signing up for courses, since there was no question of dropping out. This was one way of making us more responsible.

Martin chose skiing. At fourteen years old, he was small for his age. A four-foot six-inch Bantam hockey player is too small. This didn't create a problem. Our parents respected our choices. They respected us.

Pascal and I continued with hockey because it was our passion—we chose it without thinking. We loved skiing, but, for both of us, our passion for the little black rubber disc was too strong, even at ten and eleven years of age. We continued to ski, but only for fun, to the consternation of my ski coach. He thought I'd have a better chance to succeed in skiing. He already envisioned me on the national team, at the Olympic Games. He didn't think I would last long in hockey.

My parents always told us that we were their greatest treasure, that we kept them young and that they enjoyed accompanying us everywhere. They were our greatest fans. When winter was over and the skiing and hockey was finished, we devoted our energy to baseball. Our parents took us everywhere. It wasn't a chore for them, even if it was tiring.

I remember a fight I had with my mother, the only one in our lives.

It was in mid-summer. It was so hot and humid that even the slightest movement was an effort. After Mom had driven us around for the whole day, we were returning from the baseball field. Getting out of the car, we brats began hollering: "It's hot, it's a beautiful day, we're going to swim in the backyard. Please make us some pizza, Mom. Pizza! Pizza! Pizza!"

While we were splashing around in the pool, yelling like Tarzans, Mom was making the pizza dough. She must have been as hot as we were, and no doubt would rather have been with us in the pool.

When the pizza was ready, she couldn't get us inside. We were having too much fun and had forgotten our hunger. She finally raised her voice and made us get out of the water and put on our pyjamas.

At that point, we should have realized that she had reached the limit of her patience. But no. We sat at the table and began laughing and yelling. She served Pascal first, and the minute she put a slice of pizza on my plate, I started shrieking and whining: "You put mushrooms on the pizza. I won't eat it. You forgot about me. You only thought about the boys. I don't want it."

Normally, Mom would make half the pizza all-dressed for the boys, and half without mushrooms for spoiled little me. Well, this time she forgot. Fatigue, no doubt.

She stood there with her spatula in the air, her lips pursed and daggers shooting from her eyes.

Martin, the reasonable big brother, snapped at me, "Just take off the mushrooms, Manon. Don't have a fit."

"No, I don't want to take them off. They're disgusting and slimy. Take them off, Mom."

It must have been fatigue that made her take the slice of pizza, squash it and throw it on the table with a huge commotion.

She was beside herself. She dropped everything there, took her car keys and ran out of the house.

I started crying: "Please don't go! I love you!" In my ten-year-old mind, I thought she was leaving us for good and that we'd never see her again. It didn't occur to me then that she wouldn't get very far, dressed in her nightgown, without any money or driver's license. I wept inconsolably. I was in despair.

After half an hour, she came back. Everything was quiet at home. We had cleaned up the mess.

We threw ourselves into each other's arms and consoled each other. At the end of our street, all alone, in the dark, she had cried as much as I had.

We all went to bed happy that our mother had returned. I slept with her that night. We talked quietly. I promised not to have any more mushroom crises, and she swore she would never leave us. Finally, we slept peacefully.

Afterwards, Mom was always careful not to put mushrooms on my pizza, my favorite dish, and I watched my mouth.

My relationship with my mother is very special. I had girl-friends my own age, of course, but Mom has always been my best friend. We are very close and confide in each other. Except for a brief period, when I was a teenager, I shared all my worries, pain and fears with her. She confided in me things that a young girl could understand. Our relationship has even improved. We are now two grown women, and our friendship is all the stronger.

Our parents gave us a lot of their time—every weekend, every vacation. And they still do, even though we are all now in our twenties.

They follow Pascal's career in the Quebec Major Junior Hockey League very closely. He plays for the Faucons, the New Jersey Devils' farm club in Sherbrooke, Quebec. They attend all his games, whether in Montreal, Drummondville or Trois-Rivières. In good weather or bad, they are in the stands.

They also try to follow my career, but the distance between us makes this difficult. Atlanta isn't exactly next door. During my first year in Atlanta, they could only visit once. Thank goodness for the telephone!

PASCAL RHÉAUME

Manon has always been my best buddy. We tell each other everything about our romances, joys and sorrows.

I remember the giggling at the table when we were little. We sat across from each other and made some pretty unappetizing faces. Dad often had to tell us to settle down.

When I didn't want to do my homework in English, I'd ask her to do it. She liked school. We called her "the brain." She had good grades in every subject.

Manon was always willing to help me with my schoolwork. She was generous, always finding time or little gifts for others.

Summer or winter, we played hockey. On the rink or in the basement. Sometimes, she'd play the coach and I was the goalie. I'd put on her leg pads and gloves and she would tell me how to do it. "Lift your glove. Get over there. Move." She would shoot as hard as she could against me and I would do everything to block the shot. We would play for hours.

We played on the same team in her last year of Peewee. I was really proud of my sister.

I wouldn't have minded getting some media attention for being Manon Rhéaume's brother. But it didn't happen. She was the one doing something special, not me. And I wasn't jealous.

I liked walking with her to the Colisée for the Quebec City International Peewee Hockey Tournament. People would recognize her and say hello. I was proud to be at her side.

It's the same today.

Manon has become a driving force for me. I never thought she would go so far. She tells me how it's going in Atlanta and encourages me to continue with the New Jersey Devils.

Who knows, maybe one day we'll be on the same team again!

MARTIN RHÉAUME

Manon and I didn't always get along perfectly.

When we were little, we were together all the time. If one Rhéaume was playing in an arena, the others were in the stands. If an uncle or an aunt wanted to see us on a Sunday afternoon, they didn't come to our house, they did a tour of the city arenas.

Pascal and I, like brothers everywhere, teased Manon. And we used to like to scare her.

She was terrified of spiders. As soon as we saw one on TV or in a book, we would call her: "Hurry Manon, come see this." She would have a nervous breakdown. We would tell her we had caught a bunch of them and we'd put them in her bed. We knew how to get her mad. But we'd stop before she told our parents.

I stopped playing hockey because I wasn't growing fast enough. I was too small for Bantam. That didn't keep me out of the game altogether, though. I helped my dad, and that way I looked after Manon a bit.

Where I really was her coach was in baseball. She was a great catcher. The technique she had developed for hockey worked well in both sports. She was also a pretty good batter.

When she was seventeen or eighteen, our relationship started to sour. I don't really know what happened. Maybe it was her delayed teenage crisis. We were like fire and water, to the point that we couldn't even speak to each other.

Fortunately, in the last two years our relationship is back on track. She's my buddy again and we talk about everything, including her new life and my upcoming marriage.

She never misses an opportunity to please me. She never forgets my birthday, sends me Valentine's Day cards, brings me baseball caps for my collection. She's the perfect sister.

If I ever have a little girl, I want her to be like Manon. I want her to be a goalie.

4

MANON PREMIERES

My Peewee career was a logical follow-up to my experience at the Atom level. I still didn't understand all the little schemes that were going on behind my back and getting in my way, but I was more aware of them. The unfairness hurt me less.

In the Atom AA training camp the next year, I worked hard, as hard as I could.

At eleven years of age, I was still not well developed, and it was not immediately obvious yet that I was a girl. One day, a man sitting in the stands who knew me well, Mr. Tanguay, challenged a scout in the next seat: "One of the six goalies down there is a girl. I bet you can't tell which!"

Well, the scout looked hard, took a couple of guesses, but if he'd been a betting man, he would have been a few bucks poorer, because try as he might to spot what he thought were feminine moves or gestures, he never found "the girl."

When I came off the ice, I headed to the dressing room to change before the guys. Mr. Tanguay stopped me and said,

"Manon, take off your mask. This guy doesn't believe you're a girl." I did what I was asked. When the scout saw the little gold circles in my pierced ears, he nearly flipped. He told me I was the only one of the six goalies who hadn't, in his opinion, shown at least some feminine gestures.

Despite my good performance, the coach cut me. I was back down in the CC category. I was really disappointed not to have made the AA league. I cried a river. I felt it was so unfair because I would have loved to have had the experience.

A few days later, my father sat me on his knee and gently told me what his friends had reported to him that the coach had said: "There's no way a girl is going to play on my team."

Pierre told me the coach had only let me come to camp as a kind of formality, and that it bothered him that I was better than the other goalies. But he had to let me go anyway because I would never be able to face up to the big tournaments—I wouldn't be able to handle the pressure.

This slap in the face discouraged me only momentarily. I dried my eyes and used this unfortunate episode to motivate myself even more. "They may think they're going to stop me, but I've wanted to play in the Quebec International Peewee Tournament for as long as I can remember, and I will. Someday they'll give in. They'll see that I am good."

Thus, I prepared myself mentally to play Peewee CC. I imagined myself as a lioness going out on the hunt for her cubs.

Happily, Pierre was the team coach. With him, I knew at least, there would be no prejudices.

My father had just taken a one-year break from coaching, content to watch the game from the stands for a while. In that way he had been able to listen in on what was being said by parents and fans about the coaches, the kids, the decisions. He'd heard a lot of hateful comments from people, and he was forced to see that the world of hockey is a jungle, a place where jealousy and scheming are common, a battlefield where the fighting never ends.

So he returned to hockey with a new coaching vision, a new approach. His choice for a new assistant coach was a psychologist, Michel Fiset. Pierre explained that he wanted help coaching a team where the kids would have fun playing hockey, and where the parents would support their children and encourage them to have fun—not play to make the adults look good! He also wanted the parents to help run the team and seek sponsorships. Michel accepted the job right away.

To select their players during the training camp, Pierre and Michel developed their own evaluation method. All the players' efforts were judged according to precise criteria and everything was marked on an evaluation sheet. This provided a fair assessment of every player, so the selection was also fair and unassailable. Players were chosen for their hockey skills, and not because Pierre or Michel knew their father or mother. This was a new way of doing things in Peewee hockey.

Pierre didn't want to get involved in the selection of goaltenders. To keep the peace and to avoid accusations of favoritism from other parents, he asked that a committee be formed to assess four of us, including me. He told us all that he would accept the committee's decision, whatever it was, and that he would be the coach whether or not I made the cut. But in the end he got what he wanted: I was chosen, along with Nicolas Savard. There wasn't a great deal of difference in our levels of competence and so it was easy to achieve fairness: we would alternate in net, no matter what happened. This principle was always respected.

Our little team worked well. The parents took their roles seriously, we had fun playing, and the results were respectable.

Then came the time for the annual Quebec Peewee Hockey Tournament. At the Peewee CC level, every game is important because only one team from each region can play in this world-renowned championship. It would all be decided by December 15, when the last regular game was to be played.

Since we were among the top teams in the standings, the parents and local Peewee hockey fans began to realize there was a chance that I would make it to the tournament. So did the reporters.

Would there be a girl in the Peewee tournament for the first time in its twenty-five years of existence? The reporters began interviewing me. And then, suddenly, all the attention focused on me.

Pierre and Michel worried that team spirit would suffer as a result. They had to pay special attention to the other players, assure them that they, too, were important.

All the media attention put a lot of pressure on our team. Naturally, the other teams were aware of the newspaper coverage, and when it came time to meet us, the game was tougher. The other team always played full out. I remember one time the tension was so high that some of my teammates were crying on the bench. An opportune time to have a professional psychologist as your assistant coach! He succeeded in calming us down and we ended up finishing first in our league.

Although there had once been a rule that all players in the Quebec City tournament had to be "of the masculine sex," this discriminatory restriction had been removed in 1980. When the standings were announced, the newspapers blared the news: "Manon Goes to Peewee Tournament, the First Girl in 25 Years." The dream I'd had since I was five years old was coming true! I, Manon Rhéaume, had dared to squeeze in through a half-open door.

As in previous years, there was a news conference at the Patro Rocamadour, a well-known recreation center in Quebec City. I was treated like a princess: helium-filled balloons, photographs, more questions from reporters. I was embarrassed to see my teammates on the sidelines.

Right after the news conference, our entire team left for a tournament in Jonquière. As I boarded the bus, I let go of all the balloons I had carefully gathered up before leaving the room. As I watched them ascend into the sky, I said, "That's for all of us. We're going to win the Jonquière tournament!"

We had a good team, but it wasn't always easy. Pierre and Michel always had to be working behind the scenes to maintain team spirit and unity.

My growing notoriety led to an offer from a hockey equipment company to supply me with sticks. My father was really pleased but told the company that for the good of the entire team and to avoid jealousy, everybody had to be included. He told them he would accept the sticks on condition that the company provide them to all my teammates, too. The company representative agreed and everybody was happy.

The rep returned one day with a goaltender's helmet. He didn't have to be a mind reader to understand that the same condition would apply: a helmet for Manon, a helmet for everyone. He found that Pierre drove a hard bargain, but for the sake of keeping peace on the team, everybody had to be "spoiled." I never got more than the others.

As the date for the Peewee tournament approached, the pressure from the media coverage increased. Again, there were conditions laid down by Pierre: when the reporters interviewed me, they also had to ask questions of the other goaltender, Nicolas Savard, and the other players. The reporters agreed, because they understood it was being done in all sincerity. Celebrity has to be shared.

The Quebec International Peewee Hockey Tournament is no small deal. It has been held annually for many years during the city's winter carnival. More than one great hockey career has got off the ground at the Quebec International Peewee Hockey Tournament: Wayne Gretzky, Guy Lafleur, Daniel Bouchard, Marcel Dionne, Gilbert Perrault.

In 1983, the first year I played in the tournament, there were 103 teams registered. About 100 others had to be refused entry by the organizers. Among the teams were twenty-two from the United States, two from Switzerland, one from France and one from Finland.

That's a lot of kids and adults to feed, lodge and organize. Traditionally, about 600 families from the Greater Quebec City region welcome the visitors into their homes, "adopting" them for two weeks. It's a wonderful experience for both hosts and guests.

On the morning of the tournament's first game, February 11, 1984, I had to answer questions from a dozen reporters. A TV crew from Toronto even came to film me. I gave radio interviews to every station in Quebec City. My participation in the tournament caused a real commotion.

What a thrill it was to step on to the ice of the Quebec City Colisée, in front of a full house applauding wildly. For an eleven-year-old, it was an indescribable experience. I practically did a backflip on the ice craning my neck to try to see where the stands ended. The spotlights blinded us. The noise was deafening.

My teammates and I looked like little zombies, with our mouths open and our eyes popping, skating with robot-like stiffness. We warmed up as best we could under the circumstances.

I can remember it all like it was just yesterday ...

I'm standing at attention, staring at the Canadian flag and listening religiously to the national anthem. Focused. Practically in a trance.

I just want the game to start. The adrenaline is pumping and if I have to stay still for another second, my legs are going to take off on their own across the ice.

Finally, the music stops and the crowd claps. I seem to hear them chanting my name.

Then, suddenly, someone signals me to skate over to the boards. Someone important wants to have his picture taken with me. I look at him. I don't know him and I couldn't give a damn about having my photo taken with him. At least if it was Quebec Nordiques coach Michel Bergeron or goalie Daniel Bouchard, my hero ... but no!

I reply, confidently, "No, I can't. It's a rule and a habit that on the day of a game, I concentrate only on the game. Nothing else." I feel the people around me grow uneasy.

My father signals me over to the team bench and says, "Manon, it's Ed Broadbent, a politician, an important man. Drop the rule for today and have your picture taken with him. You can get your concentration back after. It won't be a problem."

So I bend the rules and submit to the photo session, trying to maintain my concentration all the same. Only eleven years old and already I'm learning to deal with media pressure before, during and after the game.

Finally, the match begins. We're playing the Indians from Hobbema, Alberta. Playing in the Colisée makes me so nervous I'm ready to snap, and I feel the same is true for my teammates. But I tell myself that the kids from Hobbema must be feeling the same way. All the strategies, all the plays that Pierre has explained to us a thousand times over are merely the vaguest memories now. We're playing by reflex.

The action has been at the other end of the rink since the first whistle. I'm getting bored and impatient. Time is dragging.

Finally, the game is coming toward me. The Indians are on the attack. A first shot and ... No way! It's in the net! I shout my encouragement to my teammates: "Let's go! Don't slack off! Let's go, guys!"

They're very nervous, I can feel it. They're jabbering away on the ice like never before.

I get a hold of myself and make some nice saves.

I feel the crowd behind me, hear their applause, see them jump to their feet when I beat the puck. They're rooting for me because I'm a girl, but I'd rather they were shouting like that strictly because of my performance.

The camera flashes are dazzling me. I try to stay focused on the game.

During the first intermission, Pierre and Michel succeed in calming us down and bringing us back to earth. We win the game 12-2. The poor opposing goalie was under fire constantly, especially from Sébastien Drapeau and Sylvain Hains, who each scored a hat trick.

We were so happy!

It was Nicolas's turn to mind the net for our second game, against the team from Lauzon, near Quebec City. Again, we won handily.

We were finally eliminated in the semifinals by another Quebec team, from Loretteville. But it was a good game that ended 3-1.

What an experience the tournament was, joyful and emotional!

There was so much media coverage that fans recognized me when I walked around the Colisée after our team was eliminated. I was shy and blushed when they asked for my autograph.

It's crazy what the media can do! A little unknown girl from Lac Beauport, a little Cinderella, becoming a princess overnight. When the media decide it's news, an ordinary life becomes a fairy tale—or a dream come true!

Recently, flipping through a scrapbook of photos and newspaper clippings that my mother has painstakingly kept up to date for me, I found an old article in *Le Progrès*

Dimanche. In it, I said after the Jonquière tournament on January 15, 1984: "One day, a woman will make the National Hockey League. If no one prevents her."

A premonition?

Maybe.

NICOLE RHÉAUME

Being a goalie's mother is much more stressful than being the mother of a regular player. And I know what I'm talking about, since I'm also a mother of regular players. I'm very nervous when I watch Manon play, but not when I'm watching Pascal or Martin play.

It's not because I'm afraid my little girl will be hurt—not at all. It's got nothing to do with being a girl, it's just the fact that playing in net is different.

When a forward makes a mistake, another forward or the defensemen can regain control of the game. But when the goalie makes a mistake, that's it. The puck goes in. The goalie is always alone in nets.

Then there's the reaction from some of the fans when a goal is scored: it's because the goalie is weak. You hear that kind of thing all the time.

It's terrible what people say about the goalie, and about Manon in particular: "What the heck is she doing in there? There are lots of guys who want to be goalie. She's stealing somebody else's place."

It hurts when I hear that.

That's why I always try to sit alone in a corner of the stands, far away from the parents of the other players and, if possible, from the other fans.

When Manon plays, I'm constantly squirming in my seat, gesturing with my hands and talking to myself. It's as though I were in her place. I'd like to help her.

Even though she's been injured a couple of times, I'm not too worried that she'll be seriously hurt, because she told me once that the noise sounds much louder in the stands than it really is. There's an echo, with the puck coming in so fast, but there's no danger.

I really want to believe her, but I'm a bit mistrustful of her pride and her ego. When she takes a hard shot, she rubs herself a bit—not long—and carries on. But she ends up with enormous and painful bruises.

I try not to think about injuries. I put myself in a shell, just like her, and I have confidence in her. I tell myself that an Olympic ski run is much more dangerous.

I've always felt sorry for goaltenders. The job carries so much weight and responsibility.

I can see her as a small child, in front of this enormous net while the other kids were playing at the other end of the rink. Alone.

If I'm nervous when Manon plays, it's only because I want her to play well. She's really alone in the net.

5

A TOUGH APPRENTICESHIP
FOR A TOUGH LADY

The world of kids' hockey is tough, competitive, aggressive and nasty. And I don't mean on the ice, where children are being children. I mean in the stands, where the adults sit. I can understand sometimes, because for some people hockey is like a drug or a religion. But some things are unacceptable—like when a man appoints himself coach of a team to be sure his son is picked. When you see all the politics, the games behind the scenes, the pettiness that can even become dangerous— well, sometimes it seems as if the world's gone a little nuts.

From the youngest age, I had to deal with all sorts of pettiness.

Generally, starting at the Atom CC level (when I began winning trophies for best goaltender), parents whose children were not directly competing with me demonstrated a lot of compassion for this little nine-year-old girl who was boldly breaking into a boys' world. They recognized my abilities and my value.

But whenever there was the least bit of jealousy, when the parents of some other goaltenders began looking too closely at my performance, they would make snide remarks to the coach to try to raise some doubt in his mind: "Yes, but she's not as experienced ... She'll crack under pressure at tournaments ... It's going to cause problems in the dressing room ... She'll be all right in Atom, but not when she gets to Peewee ... She's taking my boy's place—he could make the NHL, and she never will ... Why waste time on a girl?"

It always took a full season to dispel the doubts. Even though they always recognized my talent in the end, at first I would have to cool my heels uselessly in a lower division. At the very least, I'd get less ice time than the other goalie.

I had to fight for my rights from a very young age. So sad. It's hard enough for a boy to deal with all the politics; I think it's twice as hard for a girl.

Happily, I didn't have to fight the battle single-handed. My parents were with me all the way. They showed me that, in this situation, there was no way to change the system and the customs; we simply had to go with the flow. Pierre fought relentlessly against all the skepticism and prejudices. He had to develop a strategy that would prove to everyone beyond a doubt that I had a place in the "marvelous world of hockey."

Every time I attended a hockey camp, Pierre insisted that the coach test me under the same conditions as the other goaltenders. He made sure that the duties were shared half-and-half with the other goalie. In this way, no one could say, "Yes, but she was in net against a weaker team ..." He didn't want to leave any room for doubt.

For the same reason, I still feel as though I always have to be at the top of my game.

When I was very young, I could go out on the rink for the sheer fun of it, just to fool around. Every player I know still does that from time to time, just to relax. That ended for me long ago: I have to be performing constantly just in case someone is watching me, checking me out, judging me.

Whether there are three, a hundred or fifteen thousand people in the stands, I always feel watched. I have to pay attention to everything I do, always do it well. Should two or three pucks get by me one after another, I find myself judged and convicted: "A real sieve! She couldn't stop a basketball."

It's been like that ever since I began to be aware of what was happening around me, ever since I was old enough to understand the unfairness I faced. Ever since Peewee, since I was thirteen years old.

As I approached my last few months in Peewee I worked extra hard, aiming for nothing less than Bantam AA. I wanted to attend Bantam AA camp, and in my mind there was no way they could demote me to CC. Not this time. Enough deceptions.

The camp went very well. Pierre Brind'Amour, a former Nordiques player, gave me a spot on his AA team. His confidence in me made me feel better, reassured me. He did it spontaneously, without hesitation and without ulterior motives. He also gave me, at least at first, as much ice time as the other goalie.

The reporters who had been following my Peewee career continued to show interest, considering that I was the first girl to play Bantam AA. And again, all the media attention proved to be a problem. It unnerved Pierre Brind'Amour a bit. After seeking the advice of my father, he applied Pierre's philosophy: to preserve team spirit, the other players had to share the spotlight. Both the sweat and the glory had to be shared.

Despite the coach's goodwill, the war of nerves escalated. The idea that I was taking the place of a future National Hockey League star began to make the rounds. Some of the parents became nastier and their remarks less subtle.

I remember one tournament in which I was selected starting goalie. All of a sudden, all hell broke loose in the stands. It was the other goalie's father, who was not buying the idea of me playing in net while his son sat out. He left the arena in a fury, ranting and raving.

Normally, I ignore what goes on in the stands, but this time there was so much racket that I would have had to be blind and deaf not to be aware of the commotion. It threw me off my game completely. I was unable to concentrate on anything other than the imaginary conversations I would have with the coach, the other goalie and, who knows, with the father himself.

It didn't scare me. At the age of fourteen I was already able to defend myself and to look out for my own interests. But I couldn't help being concerned by what had happened. After all, the father concerned was the director of the league— Pierre Brind'Amour's boss, in other words. But, luckily for me, Pierre had seen plenty of this kind of thing before. He gave me my chance for as long as he could.

The negativism of certain people sometimes verged on sheer nastiness.

"Even as a very small child, you could already see her main personality traits: a giggler, curious, a go-getter, smart."

–Pierre Rhéaume

I remember all the hurdles I had to leap, the taboos I demolished. I remember the pain and suffering I endured without shedding a tear, so that no one could call me a crybaby little girl.

My mother would have preferred that I take up figure skating, gymnastics or ballet. But no, I was already too passionate about hockey.

I can do it Daddy! Please? Let me be your goalie!

When I couldn't be in nets, I played defence.

Here I am with my little team. My dad really believed playing hockey would be just a passing fancy for me.

How proud I was to have my picture taken with Peter Stastny.

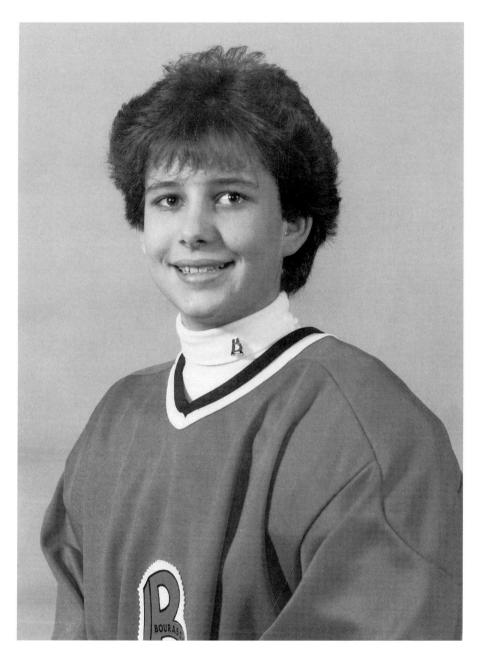

"This little girl created her own luck. She set her own goal and achieved it."

–Pierre Rhéaume

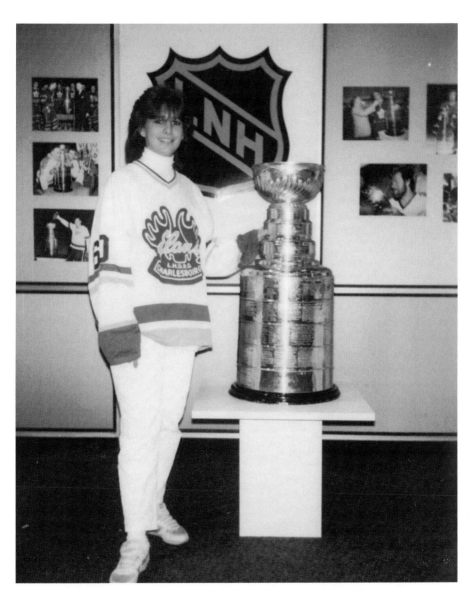

My dream wasn't to play in the National Hockey League. That was
unthinkable in those days. My dream was simply to play hockey.

My battle was to convince people to let me improve and
develop, just like the other players.

It used to happen sometimes—and I would always hear about it through the grapevine—that players on the opposing team would be told to shoot for my face, in particular around my eyes. Or even to run into me and drive me into the net. They wanted to scare me.

Anything goes to win the game. Some of the players took this maxim so much to heart that they thought of nothing else. It was ridiculous. My father suggested a trick to defend myself: support my stick against the back of the net and point the other end at the most sensitive part of the male anatomy. But I never did it. Why try to avenge myself? Because the bottom line was that while they were thinking up ways to hurt me, they weren't concentrating on their game. In the end, the coaches who counselled such behavior helped us win because, rather than focusing on their overall game strategy, the players were focusing on one opposing player—me. Me, who fears no puck. It was not a smart ploy on their part.

In my second Bantam year, 1987, the pressure from outside no doubt had something to do with the fact that I found myself warming the bench more often than not. I was getting a lot less ice time than the other goalie.

Pierre Brind'Amour must have felt manacled by the custom that there are no girls at the next level up, Midget AAA. It was unthinkable. After all, there was a girls' ringette league. Well-organized, too! Why not develop the talent of a girl there, since she was not going to go any farther in the men's leagues anyway? Let's spend our energy on the guys, who at least have a chance of moving up.

My reaction to this kind of prejudice was to work all the harder to show everyone just how wrong their thinking was. I played so well that a Junior A scout attending a tournament during his search for a Midget-level goalie put me on his draft list. He looked genuinely sorry later when he had to scratch my name. He liked my moves, my style, my reflexes. But once he realized that there was a girl behind the mask, he knew there was no chance she would play in the Midget AAA league. There was nothing he could do. Sorry!

The never-ending battle!

There are no rules or regulations requiring that Bantam AA goalies be invited to Midget AAA training camp. It's simply customary. But I certainly wasn't invited. I guess I shouldn't have been surprised.

Resigned, I attend the Midget AA camp. One of the goaltending spots had already been filled. There was one left, and my competition was a boy who had just been sent down from AAA. The team directors agreed to give me a chance to prove to them that I could do the job, but it was a waste of time. Their minds were made up. I wasn't going to play for this team.

More tears were spilled. My mother even told me, "Listen, Manon. This is crazy. Give it up. You can't go any higher."

That shook me. Me, stop? Now? I'm not ready to stop. I decided to continue, but in CC, not much more than a fun league.

I was discouraged. It was beginning to dawn on me that maybe they were all right—maybe I couldn't go any further.

At this point, in 1988, the entire province of Quebec was glued to its television sets watching a weekly soap opera called "Lance et compte" ("He Shoots, He Scores"), all about the trials and tribulations of a hockey team. At school, we talked about nothing else. The kids really identified with the stars and believed in all their stories.

I got the idea that if Réjean Tremblay, writer for "Lance et compte" and a sports reporter at the Montreal daily newspaper *La Presse*, would write into his script a girl invited to a top-level training camp, it might give girls following in my footsteps a better chance. The idea would no longer be new, because it was on TV. Maybe it would become acceptable.

I called *La Presse* and told the receptionist that I was writing something for school and needed to contact Réjean Tremblay. Amazingly, she gave me his home number in Montreal and I got in touch with him.

He agreed it wasn't a bad idea, but he saw it more as a girl who cut her hair like a boy and acted like one, fooling everyone right up until the point where, in the dressing room ...

That wasn't my idea at all. I wanted a girl who looked like a girl and who was treated like any other player.

We didn't agree, but he still found the concept intriguing. He agreed to meet me the next time he traveled to Quebec City, telling me how and where to reach him. But I called him at his hotel several times and never managed to meet him. I sent a registered letter to *La Presse*, to be sure he'd receive it. He never replied. I let it drop. I guess I was never meant to be a screenwriter, and I decided instead to be content with playing on my little fun team.

Midget CC is not really serious hockey. Often, only six or seven players showed up for practices. The players would arrive five minutes ahead of time, not really even warming up. They'd make a special effort for the real games, though, getting to the arena at least ten minutes before the match.

I tried to look for the silver lining. At least I was playing hockey.

Then came the day we were getting ready for a tournament in Sherbrooke, Quebec. The players' main concern was organizing the party after the first game on Friday night. "We'll have a blast. I know a place where the girls hang out, the music is good and the beer's cheap."

I could already see what would happen. There I'd be in net on the Saturday morning surrounded by players with headaches and shaky legs. I wasn't too excited about playing goal for a bunch of guys that couldn't even stay on their feet. I didn't want to look like an idiot. I had invested too much effort in hockey to go to Sherbrooke and look like a clown.

I decided to explain my point of view to the coach. He was furious—luckily, not at me. He had a little talk with the players, who found themselves with a problem: one of them was going to have to take my place in net. They weren't too keen.

When I saw my teammates caring more about the party than the game, I knew I'd rather quit.

I stopped playing the very week I turned seventeen. My season was finished and I had closed the book on hockey. Quit. I'd lost my spirit.

I had to give up all my dreams.

In a flash, everything I had experienced passed through my mind's eye—all the bad times and all the nastiness. I thought about the day I was refused entry into Midget AA because I was a girl. I felt like I was really at a dead end.

I had run into similar roadblocks before, but I'd always told myself I had to keep going, that I could remove the obstacle and get where I wanted to go. But this time there was no side road, no detour.

Suddenly everything in my life had changed. I felt like a different person. Rebellion aged me all of a sudden. I was transformed from a sensible little girl, lively but not troublesome, into an adolescent in crisis.

My mother, who was always my confidante, no longer recognized me. I never talked to her any more. I kept my secrets to myself. From one day to the next, I started fighting with my brother Martin, with whom I had always gotten along famously. If he said black, I'd say white.

It was a difficult time in my life, but it gave me an opportunity to try new things.

My time had always been divided between school and hockey practices. The few friends I had from school had tried hard to drag me along with them to their discos, but they were wasting their time. All these years, all I wanted to do was get to bed early so that I would be rested for the practice or game the next day. A real nun. I had no time to party, and so I often found myself all alone.

In all those years when I was surrounded by boys, I never had any boyfriends. Quite simply, I wasn't interested.

Anyway, there was no question of having a crush on one of my teammates: nothing worse for wrecking the mood in a group, for causing chaos among the guys. Even less possible was the notion of being courted by an opponent. These lofty principles considerably narrowed my field of suitors.

The first boy I ever hung around with other than when I was playing hockey was called Steve. I met him when I was about sixteen.

Steve and I were always together. He was a hockey player, but since he no longer played competitively, it was no problem. We spent evenings together watching the Nordiques on television, or even better, at the Colisée, where we could see the action from up close.

My parents never questioned my comings and goings. They let me live my life. As long as my school marks were good, I had all the freedom I wanted.

By now I was attending Sainte-Foy Junior College, near Quebec City, and my studies went well. I earned a diploma in humanities. I was thinking of entering the communications field, or even teaching. But destiny decided to change my career plans.

NICOLE RHÉAUME

Not just anyone can become a goalie. You have to have a very special character to put up with the pressure. You have to be very independent. It takes someone who is capable of great concentration, who can play in a bubble and shut out distractions.

Manon has always been like that. Often she would go up to her room, close the door, put on some music and read. She played a lot by herself with her imaginary friends. She could spend hours playing or studying without being distracted by things, always concentrating hard on what she was doing. When it was time to study, she focused totally on studying. When it was time for hockey, she focused totally on that. There are no halfway efforts with Manon. Because she can concentrate so intensely, she succeeds in everything she undertakes.

I am very proud of Manon. I am proud of the woman she has become and of the way her career is going.

Manon is a winner.

Manon and I have almost always been very close. She would tell me everything, just like a friend. I would tell her the things a little girl could understand.

When she fell in love for the first time, she distanced herself from me. She didn't talk to me any more. It was as though I didn't exist. After a year and half, she broke up with the boy and I got my friend back. Everything was just like before: sharing the secrets, joys and lots of laughter.

After that, her romances never affected our relationship. The little girl had become a woman. All of a sudden. Then she could separate the different parts of her life without getting them all mixed up. She would open one door and close another and life went on without any big upsets.

We still share secrets.

6

AND WHY NOT GIRLS?

Almost a year had passed since I quit my Midget CC team, and I was missing hockey. A passion will always remain a passion.

It had been difficult to completely eliminate hockey from my life, because I was always inside arenas cheering my brother Pascal and his team. The more I watched them play, the more I felt the deep desire to get on the ice.

One fine day, someone told me that a hockey training camp for women would be held at Laval University in Quebec City. I went to take a look. The calibre of play was way below that of the guys, and I didn't really feel like trying out.

Two of the girls on the Laval team, Diane Michaud and Paulette Cormie, also played for Sherbrooke in Quebec's Eastern Townships region. Seeing that I wasn't exactly moved by the thought of playing for Laval, they invited me to try out for Sherbrooke.

Why not?

Things were different in Sherbrooke. The players were top-notch. I liked the coach and there was a nice feeling about the team. They painted me a glowing picture of how we would win the provincial, Canadian and—who knows?—world championships. Also, there was already discussion of women's hockey being accepted as an official sport for the Winter Olympics that were coming soon.

To really get the best out of myself, I have to have goals to shoot for. The more pressure, the better I perform. Finally, I had found a new goal to pursue: the Olympics!

Although I'd rediscovered a desire to play, my body had its own ideas. I was not in shape. Since my "retirement" from Midget, I hadn't been involved in any sports activities at all.

I put the pedal to the floor and had a ball playing with my new friends for the entire year. I renewed my love affair with the puck and my morale was steady. My passion for hockey had returned stronger than ever.

We were practicing once or twice a month in Sherbrooke and playing weekly in our league in Repentigny, near Montreal. Two and a half hours there and back was a long way to go just to practice, but I had no choice.

Nicole often came with me to Repentigny. She didn't like to see me out on the roads at such late hours. We had the rink from eight o'clock to midnight, but it wasn't unusual for a game to finish at two in the morning. When you play for a women's league, you take whatever ice time is available.

I developed a case of mononucleosis from burning the candle at both ends. The doctors insisted I rest for a month, but thanks to Nicole and her own special health diet (fruits, fresh vegetables, calf's liver), I was back on my feet in two weeks.

We had an exhibition game scheduled against a team from the media, and I wouldn't have missed that for the world!

I'd made a lot of contacts from spending so much time in arenas, either playing or watching Pascal play. I knew just about all the main players, coaches and scouts in the province. There wasn't much that got by me. I knew all the players' ages and the teams they had played for. I knew beforehand when players were about to be picked up by a team.

I minded my own business, but I saw and heard a lot.

One day, when our entire family was in Drummondville to watch Pascal play, Donald Marier, the scout for the Trois-Rivières Draveurs of the Quebec Major Junior Hockey League, a man I spoke to a lot, introduced me to Trois-Rivières head coach Gaston Drapeau.

We had never really spoken, but he knew me vaguely and had been following my progress. I told him I was really unhappy about not being invited to the Midget AAA training camp but that I was getting ready for the Canadian women's championships a few months down the road. I also told him how difficult I found it to perform well with only one practice session a week.

Gaston offered to let me train with his team in Trois-Rivières. It would give me a chance to get a bit more ice time and to play a bit at the Junior A level.

I didn't even think about it for two seconds before pouncing on the opportunity.

On the day of the first practice, I rose at dawn to be in Trois-Rivières at 8:00 a.m. I was really excited. My dad suggested he come with me. It was a nice gesture, but no way! I was the one who had arranged this chance and I didn't want anyone to think that he had won a favor for me.

At the Trois-Rivières arena, Gaston showed me my changing room and asked me if I was nervous. "Me, nervous? No. Just happy! I can hardly wait to get on the ice."

The practice started and the players shot softly ... gently. After twenty minutes, they were still firing creampuffs at me. I yelled, "Okay, you guys, I'm warmed up now. Now you can try some real shots."

They started picking up the pace until finally they were no longer holding back and were shooting as usual.

I practiced with them a few times, and it proved to be helpful. My game improved a lot and I was a more effective player for the women's team.

That year, 1991, our Sherbrooke women's team won the provincial championships in Bromont and finished second to the Ontario team in the Canadian championships in Montreal. I was proud to be awarded the trophy for the best goaltender of the national series.

It was a wonderful experience. I knew I had the chance to make the team for the 1992 world championships in Finland, so I decided to stay with the Sherbrooke team the following year.

Meanwhile, Gaston Drapeau was keeping an eye on me.

At the end of the 1991 season, a new men's team, the Jaguars, was to be formed for the Level II League in Louiseville, a little town near Trois-Rivières, midway between Montreal and Quebec City. Yves Beaudry, coach of the team, who had heard about my practice sessions with the Trois-Rivières Draveurs, invited me to a camp in May. There, he would select the first round of players who would go to the real camp at the start of the season, in August. He also invited my brother Pascal.

Our parents came with us to Louiseville for the camp, which was to last several days. From day one it was obvious that Pascal would be going further. But there were five other goalies and I was in a fierce battle to make the cut. I had to show them everything I had.

To save a bit of money, we had taken one hotel room with two large beds. The first night, Pascal snored up a storm. When he starts, there's nothing you can do to stop him. I shook him as hard as I could, kicked his mattress, but it was no use. I didn't sleep a wink all night.

It showed the next day on the ice. So much so that coach Beaudry asked my father, "What's the matter with Manon? She played well yesterday, but she seems tired today and her reflexes are slower."

My dad replied, "Pascal snored all night and Manon didn't get any sleep. I know it sounds like an excuse. You can take it for what it's worth."

"Well," the coach said, "in any case, tomorrow we'll put her in more than the others to be really sure that she's giving it her best shot. If we keep her, we want to be sure we're not making a mistake. You make sure she sleeps well tonight."

A little family shuffle was required. I would sleep with Nicole, Pascal with Pierre, and everybody wore earplugs.

We all slept like logs, and at breakfast we were rested and chipper. Everyone else around the table was in a good mood, but I was lost in my thoughts. It had suddenly dawned on me that this camp was my last chance. It was now or never. If it turned out badly, I would drop the whole idea of playing in a men's league and never discuss it again. I wasn't kidding, either. It was make it or break it time.

Beaudry had enlisted two goaltending judges to help him in his selection. I really believe I was at my best: great glove saves, butterfly stops, shifting my weight, moving the puck around, controlling the game around the net, talking to my defensemen in an authoritative tone. I showed them what I could do.

The judges said, "That's fine, she's in. Not only is her technique better than the others' but she's smart, too. We can do something with her for sure."

You can't possibly imagine the joy I felt when they said that. The impossible dream wasn't over yet!

After the final draft in June, Pascal made the Draveurs and I had the slightly lesser honor of joining the Louiseville Jaguars. It was the first time a girl had made it that far. The coaches laughed at first, but they ended up applauding.

For the summer, my father had reserved ice time to allow Pascal and me to train. We also joined a fitness club to improve our cardiovascular systems.

When I arrived at the Louiseville training camp in August, I knew that all my hard work during the summer had paid off. I had a new feeling of confidence and of being in full possession of my faculties.

Coach Drapeau, who wanted to invite me to the Draveurs' camp, came to Louiseville to take a look. I guess he wanted to reassure himself. Finally, he decided he would invite me to help my development. Luck was with me—a chance to attend a Junior A camp! There was no way I was going to let this chance pass me by.

Only two goalies would make the cut at the Draveurs' camp, and I knew ahead of time that I would not be one of them. I was going for the experience and the fun.

The Draveurs camp went well. The angels were with me. But during one practice, I had to make an extra effort to stop a shot by Yannic Perreault, who had just been drafted by the Toronto Maple Leafs and who I thought was good. I really wanted to stop his shot and I managed to do so by doing the splits. But I hurt myself, pulling a muscle in my thigh.

I didn't say anything to anybody. There was no way I was going to pull out just because of an injury.

In my next appearance, during an exhibition game against the Saint-Jean Lynxes, I made another abrupt move which tore my hamstring muscle. The coach had to pull me midway through the game because I couldn't go on.

Then the gossip started: "Was she really hurt or was she just not good enough? Was she too nervous? Maybe the coach didn't think she could do it."

Incredible! People can be so mean! Normally, I would never have played with an injury like that. I knew I was taking a big risk, but I couldn't pass on an opportunity to play in a Junior A exhibition game.

I was on crutches for the next two weeks, and not just for show. My leg was black from hip to toe. It wasn't very pretty, but I wore Bermuda shorts all the same to stop the wagging tongues.

What was important was that I had shown Beaudry and Drapeau what I could do. Beaudry took me for the Louiseville team and Drapeau named me third-string goalie for the Draveurs.

So I went to live in Trois-Rivières. I rented a little studio apartment and enrolled at Trois-Rivières Junior College to finish the last few courses I needed for my humanities diploma.

Since Pascal was playing with the Draveurs, I didn't feel so alone, so far from home.

Pascal was boarding in a private home with another player on his team, Claude Poirier. Since I was often at my brother's place and they were always together, Claude soon became more than a friend. He became my second boyfriend.

At the beginning, I didn't want anyone to know about us. I was afraid they would say, "Manon's dating a guy from the Draveurs." But since we were always together, everyone found out. Fortunately, the guys were very respectful and minded their own business. They knew me and knew very well that I wasn't the kind of girl to hop from one guy to another. At nineteen I was no scatterbrain, and I was big enough to know what I was doing.

I had to rest for two and a half months to recover from my thigh injury. I couldn't even do my fitness routine. So when I started practicing again I really had to work hard to catch up to the other goalies. I also had to start thinking about my Sherbrooke women's team and the fast-approaching world championships in Finland.

Two weeks after my return to the ice, I was once again called into the media spotlight.

One of the Draveurs' goalies was injured. As I was still one of their back-up goalies, they called me to dress.

I warmed the bench for one game, then another, but in the third they threw me into the thick of the action. It was November 26, 1991. The other goalie had blown a 5-1 lead, allowing four goals. The game had to be turned around, and it was up to me to do it.

In the middle of the second period, cold, I stepped onto the ice, distracted by the cameras that had been following me since the first game. There was an ovation from the crowd when the fans recognized me skating toward the net, and that didn't do much to calm my nerves! I knew the fans would expect a lot. Their judgment on this performance would be final. There would be no second chance.

In the middle of the third period, I took a shot in the face that broke the grille on my mask. The hit cut my eyebrow, but I didn't even notice it right away. It wasn't until I started having trouble seeing that I realized I was bleeding. The officials stopped the game and I skated over to the bench to clean my face. But it was bleeding too profusely and I needed stitches. The coach pulled me from the game.

The gossipmongers started wagging their tongues right away: "Naturally—she's a girl. She should go play with her dolls."

That was the beginning and the end of my Junior A experience, because I never again had a chance to fill in for the other two goalies. But I had the honor of becoming the first woman to tend goal in the Quebec Major Junior Hockey League.

The reporters leapt on the story, and that's really when the media circus began. Since then, they've never let me be.

Coach Drapeau tried to help me, but he was quickly overwhelmed. Never had he imagined so many calls, requests for interviews and meetings.

He turned for help to his friend Pierre Lacroix, a manager of athletes, who advised him to seek professional help. So he called NATIONAL Public Relations of Montreal to help us manage this media avalanche.

I returned to my team in Louiseville, which wasn't doing well. We were in the cellar in the standings. The coach had been fired and his successor didn't give me much ice time. I was the third-string goalie. I felt underused and no longer very motivated.

But the training camp was approaching for selection of the members of the women's national team that would travel to Finland to represent Canada.

I thought it made more sense to return to my Sherbrooke team after the Christmas holidays, in order to readjust to the pace of the women's game and their shooting. That year, 1992, we won the Quebec championships and the bronze medal at the Canadian championships.

The national women's team camp was held in Kitchener, Ontario. All went smoothly and seven Quebecers were named to the team, including six from Sherbrooke: Marie-Claude Roy, France Saint-Louis, Nathalie Picard, Danielle Goyette, Nancy Drolet and me. We were all very proud.

On April 12, the team took off from Toronto for Finland.

I was really excited to be going to compete against the best women hockey players in the world. It was also my first trip to Europe. We were jubilant!

We spent the first week in the little village of Veramake, a few hundred kilometers from Tempere, site of the world championships. We needed this week of seclusion to build team spirit. We didn't even know one another, hailing as we did from all over Canada; nor had we ever played together. We needed to become familiar with each other and become a real team as quickly as possible.

Our coaches—Rick Polutnik, Sharon Miller and Pierre

Charette—took care of business. They made us switch room-mates every day, because sharing a room is the fastest way to get to know someone. It was a lot of fun.

We practiced twice a day, in the arena and outdoors. The coaches organized all sorts of games to help us get to know each other. They also gave us relaxation courses to help us concentrate.

The results were amazing. The girls were happy, the team was unified, and everyone got along. There were no little cliques, no jealousies. We were really pumped, and there was no question in anyone's mind that we would return from the tournament with the gold medal.

After our week of training, we traveled to Tempere, where my mother was waiting for me. She wasn't going to miss my appearance in the world championships.

Mom had been in Finland for a whole week, but we hadn't been able to see each other. We had been living like real recluses in Veramake. But she had taken the opportunity to travel around the country and have a good time with my Aunt Mireille, who was also keen to see me play.

When our bus finally arrived at the hotel in Tempere, Mom and I leapt into each other's arms. We were so happy to see each other again. It had been a tiring week of training and I needed to be coddled.

The five other girls from Sherbrooke felt the same way, and they embraced my mother as if she were theirs. Being able to speak Quebec French with her was just what the doctor ordered for their homesickness. We had lived in English the entire week and it was a relief not to have to search for words for once.

We got our hotel rooms and rested for a few hours before quickly returning to our training regimen.

The arena where we were practicing was a real fortress. Spectators were not allowed—not even the parents of the foreign players. My mother and Aunt Mireille went through every kind of song and dance, but the soldiers at the gates wouldn't be cajoled into letting them in. They were absolutely inflexible. Orders are orders. To see us, they had to wait at the hotel for us to return from practice—in the lobby! Not even our parents were allowed up to our rooms.

So that we could have a bit of privacy, Mom and Aunt Mireille would invite me to eat with them right near their hotel. They had found a really good pizzeria and they knew I would appreciate that. We talked for hours about their trip and about my week in training. It was great to be together again!

The atmosphere was electric; team spirit was strong. Unfortunately, it was hard to get to know the girls from the other countries, since we were practicing at different times and contact was extremely restricted.

I found I was once again a bit of a celebrity. The European reporters had heard about me, and one of the Swiss players even sought me out to see what I looked like. I was flabbergasted!

The tournament went very well. In fact, the calibre of playing among the opposition wasn't very high. The teams didn't seem to be all that experienced.

I rotated goaltending duties with Marie-Claude Roy and we won every game. When the semifinals began, the coach decided to put me in net full-time.

The Japanese team, our first opponents, fought hard. They wanted very badly to win but they just weren't technically strong enough. The game only started to get interesting near the end.

Next, we met the home team, Finland. There was much more action this time, but we still won easily enough, 6-2.

The Americans won their semifinal game just as easily.

In the finals, Sweden would meet Finland for the bronze medal and Canada and the United States would fight for the gold. Now it was time for the real action.

The Americans were really confident when they arrived at the arena. Like us, they had won all their games, but their goal total was higher.

A thundering sound filled the stands. There wasn't an empty seat in the house. The Finnish team had just beaten the Swedes in front of a home crowd and the fans were joyous. Adding to the party-like atmosphere was a group of girls from Toronto who had come just to support us, shouting their encouragement. Their faces were all made up in red and white, with maple leafs and CANADA spelled out. Little Canadian flags were flying in all corners of the arena. These girls had even managed to make up the face of Mr. Didduck, the father of one of the girls on the team. With his white hair and booming voice, he added quite a lot to the revelry in the stands.

The crowd seemed to be on our side.

As it turned out, the Americans were not as strong as we had anticipated. Even though they were the toughest team we had faced so far, it was still an easy win. I felt completely relaxed and I was aiming right away for a shutout. And that's exactly what we got: 8-0. A real cakewalk!

As is customary, we shook our opponents' hands after the game. The Americans were looking a bit sheepish. It seems they'd been mentally mounting the winners' podium as soon as they'd walked into the arena.

We were surrounded with goodwill. The fans applauded us wildly. They had adopted us. Suddenly, "O Canada" was playing. I was very emotional, with a lump in my throat and my eyes filled with tears.

The victory party that followed lasted all night, and the next morning we boarded the plane for home exhausted and with circles under our eyes, but every one of us with a smile on our lips.

I needed two weeks to recover from my trip.

I really loved my European experience and the opportunity to discover another culture, another way of life. Finnish cuisine is excellent, but it's always a surprise to see fish on the menu for breakfast—not exactly your basic North American bacon, eggs and toast. And their pastries and ice cream are to die for! For a food lover like me, living over there would be torture, because I would have to maintain control at all times. I'm really afraid of putting on weight.

Finland's towns are pretty and clean. People are proud of their homes and maintain them impeccably. I never saw anything run-down.

Something else that struck me was the mutual respect between pedestrians and drivers. Pedestrians cross the street only at intersections—not like here, where everyone runs into the traffic wherever and whenever they want.

I finished the 1992 season with the Sherbrooke women's team. I wasn't waiting for men's hockey to come and find me.

Destiny would follow its course.

And I would let it ride.

GASTON DRAPEAU,
COACH, TROIS-RIVIÈRES DRAVEURS

As a former resident of Quebec City, I had read about Manon in the newspapers. In her Peewee days, she got so much coverage you couldn't help but know of her. We met in arenas a few times but nothing more.

It was my scout, Donald Marier, who introduced us. When I heard she wanted more opportunities to practice before the Canadian women's championships, I didn't wait to invite her to join us for some sessions. That seemed to please her.

When she showed up at the Trois-Rivières arena, I went out to meet her in the parking lot. Like any gentleman, I offered to carry her equipment bag. She declined. I guess she's got hockey in her blood so much that she accepts everything that goes along with it, like carrying her own bag. And God knows, the goalie's bag is the heaviest on the team.

At the start of the practice, the guys didn't dare shoot with full force. She had to insist before she started getting the real shots. I took out my camera so she could analyze her style later. I was impressed. She has mastered some technical points that a lot of Junior A players have not.

Because of her talent and her technical abilities, I invited her to the Draveurs' training camp the next summer. I did it for her, as I had for other young people in Chicoutimi who wanted to get a feel for Junior A, and as I will again for anyone who plays well.

Manon wasn't outclassed by anyone. On the contrary, she stacked up well with the other good goalies because of her attention to detail. Unlike most players, she's always ready to correct the slightest fault. She is a perfectionist.

At the time, I was convinced that she had no interest in professional hockey. I thought all she wanted was to be picked for the national team to go to the world championships, and eventually to the Olympics. She was in the right place at the right time. Good luck can help a lot.

I didn't select her as third-string goalie out of charity. She deserved it. She went through the voting process like lots of other players. Any team could have picked her.

She took part 100 percent in every team activity: running, exercises on and off the ice, exhibition games. We stopped seeing her as a woman and saw her instead as just a player. She fit in completely, and we learned to get along with her.

Manon has remained very realistic. She's never wanted to take anyone else's place. She's never done anything to attract attention to herself.

Some people are very critical of her. It's too bad to see that mentality. Fortunately, it's just a small minority who think that way—people who would like to be in her place but don't have the talent or the character. Those who have known her for some time, who have watched her development and the sacrifices she's had to make, are very pleased for her.

We knew, of course, that people would be intrigued and that the media would talk about her, but we never imagined to what degree. The only thing that counted for her was hockey—not showmanship.

I could have put her in a game well before November 26. During a game in Saint-Jean, Quebec, lots of media were there behind my bench. There were two minutes left and we were leading 4-1. The reporters asked me to put her in. I didn't want to. I wouldn't have done it for another goalie, so why would I for Manon? For show? For the cameras? I wasn't interested.

When I put her in net against the Granby Bisons, it was to turn the game around. The other goalie was playing badly and had let in too many goals. I put Manon on the ice, as I would have put in any other goalie. It was the right decision.

It takes quite a personality to stand in front of the net when you know everyone is watching and judging you. If the young guys in Junior A had even half as much character as she did, more of them would make it to the NHL.

She injured her eye in the middle of the third period. So? It could have happened to anyone. After that, the media wouldn't ease up.

Being in Phil Esposito's farm club is a good thing for both of them.

Phil Esposito is a smart man. He saw that she had media appeal. He also understood that she had potential and that she wouldn't embarrass his team. He took Manon, offering in return to make her greatest dream come true: to play hockey and see how far she could go with her passion.

Manon is very much aware of the effects of this whole story on her. She has persevered because she likes to play hockey. That's all. She is prepared to face the media to go as far as she can.

7

THE TAMPA BAY CAMP

During the summer of 1992, I worked in Montreal for the Réseau des sports, RDS (the French-language equivalent of TSN). I was a "gofer," doing a little bit of everything for the network.

All of a sudden, there were rumors going around concerning me. At 6:30 one morning a reporter called me to ask if it was true that the Ottawa Senators of the NHL had invited me to their training camp. After that, the telephone didn't stop ringing all day.

I had never been in contact with anyone from the Ottawa organization. I didn't have a clue what was going on.

But at about this time, without my knowing it, Jacques Campeau, the scout for the newest entry into the NHL, the Tampa Bay Lightning, had sent team director Phil Esposito a videocassette of me in action.

Jacques wanted Phil to take a look at me and make a judgment without knowing I was a girl. What Esposito said was:

"A little small for a goalie, but he moves well. He has good reflexes. We can invite him to camp." When he was informed of my gender, his first reaction was: "She plays like a goalie. Why not invite her, just like the other guys we invite? Then we'll really see what she's got."

A bit later in the summer, I was at the Montreal Forum with RDS as they did a story on the NHL draft. All the team owners, scouts and managers arrived for the annual "auction." There, Jacques Campeau introduced me to Phil Esposito.

Esposito asked me if I was really interested in coming to a professional hockey training camp. I guess he saw the twinkle in my eye, because he quickly added, "I'm going to mail you an invitation. If you're interested, just fill out the forms and send them back to me as quickly as possible."

A few weeks later, as promised, I received the invitation and quickly completed the papers. I was taking a chance. So were the Tampa Bay people.

They didn't even wait for the start of the camp to bring me to Tampa Bay. I was invited to one of their very first promotional events: they had invited the public to visit their new arena and learn all about the game of hockey.

As you might imagine, hockey is pretty foreign to Florida. A game on ice is a new phenomenon. People can talk for hours about basketball, football or baseball, but hockey is not in their genes the way it is with people from Montreal or Quebec City. You even have to warn them to keep their eye glued to the puck, because you have to pay attention if you want to follow a puck that's going 100 miles an hour.

This was also the day for the Tampa Bay organization to introduce the players to the public. I stopped a few shots. I didn't do too badly, either, which reassured everyone. They could now rest easy until the opening of the training camp in September.

For the rest of the summer, I trained hard to be in top shape for the camp. Come September 10, I didn't want to be taken for a weak female.

The fateful day dawned. After picking up the last of my things in Chicoutimi, I headed out of town for a week with my duffel bag and clothes, my spirit soaring and with stars in my eyes. I was really happy ... but I remained realistic: this was a training camp, and there were no guarantees. This was a terrific life experience—no more.

My brother Pascal had been called to New Jersey for the training camp of the New Jersey Devils, and my parents were very upset that my camp in Tampa Bay was being held at the same time. We did the only sensible thing: my mother came with me to Florida and my father accompanied Pascal to New Jersey.

I would really have liked to have been on the same plane as my mother, because I'm afraid of flying. But it wasn't possible. Fortunately, the Chicoutimi-Montreal leg went well. But things went downhill after that.

The Tampa Bay organization changed my flight at the last minute and I had to make a stopover in New York City. During the stopover, a huge storm blew up: winds, lightning, thunder—the whole nine yards. A real deluge. The takeoff for Tampa Bay was already an hour behind schedule when the airline decided to corral all the passengers and take us to Kennedy Airport for another flight. You can't imagine the chaos!

It took a ridiculous amount of time to find everyone and put us on a bus for the other airport. I spent the day in New York, stressed out of my mind. I kept telling myself: "This can't be happening. My first day at camp and I'm going to be late. What is Phil Esposito going to think? What will the guys say?"

Finally, we took off from New York. There was a lot of turbulence at the beginning, which didn't do a lot to calm my nerves. Happily, the flight wasn't too bad after that, though.

We finally arrived in Tampa Bay, several hours late.

My mother was as nervous as I was. My original flight was supposed to have arrived only a few minutes after hers. She had been waiting for me for hours. She knew about the big storm and had been imagining all sorts of horrible things. Happily, she was with Guylaine Campion, a television reporter from Quebec, and her cameraman, and the two of them did their best to reassure her.

Everybody was relieved when I arrived. But I was freaking out to be arriving late for my first day at camp! To add to the stress, my baggage hadn't arrived with me. The evidence was there—or not there, I guess you could say—for all to see when we went to the baggage carousel: no hockey bag, no clothing. The baggage had been misdirected in New York to God knows where.

So there I was in Tampa Bay with nothing but Bermuda shorts, sweater, sandals and a purse. We had hardly said a word to one another, my mother, Guylaine, the cameraman and I, when a car from the Lightning organization arrived to take me to the hotel, where the team was meeting for the first time.

Everybody had already taken a seat, but luckily, the meeting had not yet started.

I naturally headed for the very back row in order not to call attention to myself. I sat between Marc Tardif and Jean Blouin, who I already knew.

There were only men in the room. Even though I'd expected it, it still hit me.

Just before starting the meeting, Terry Crisp, the coach, looked at me and said, "You there, in the last row! You're too far back. Move up front, there's lots of room."

Nightmare! I'm so shy. I had to get up, walk down the aisle, pass in front of everyone, feeling the eyes of the guys on me. I wanted to disappear. I was hoping that my red face wasn't shining too brightly.

The meeting finally started, but I was only half there. While Crisp talked and explained how the camp would be organized, my mind wouldn't stop working overtime. I was asking myself what I was doing there. I would have liked to have known what the guys were thinking!

I didn't regret coming, but it sure felt weird to be the only girl in the room. These weren't kids sitting beside me, they were men. Some of them I recognized from going to the Colisée in Quebec City to watch them play for the Nordiques: Tony McKegny, Basil McRae, Daniel Vincelette—guys thirty years old. Here I was in the same room with them, going to the same training camp. A professional hockey camp. That I was in a bit of a daze is about the only way I can describe it.

Nevertheless, I managed to absorb the fact that throughout the first week of camp we would be playing games. Nothing but games and no practice sessions. Kind of a four-team tournament.

There were eight goalies all together, or two per team. I was assigned to the Blues along with Wendell Young, a former Pittsburgh Penguins goalie who was wearing a Stanley Cup ring. His smile was a tad mocking but his blue eyes inspired confidence in me. We got along right away.

The meeting ended and we all went to our rooms, with visions of making the team dancing in our heads.

There was a message waiting for me with the receptionist: "No baggage tonight, but tomorrow morning for certain."

I was wondering, "Why me? I'm the only girl, I arrive late because of the plane, and now no baggage. All guaranteed to draw attention to me."

My mother had received permission from the team to room with me. The Tampa Bay people knew that I would be under considerable media pressure, and that the reporters also wanted to interview my mother. It was very reassuring to have her there with me. Remember, I was only twenty years old. But all the same, I had carefully explained to her before we left Quebec that she couldn't be there all the time. I had to mix with the group as much as possible.

The next morning, still no baggage. I was still in my Bermuda shorts and sandals. Under normal circumstances that wouldn't have been so bad, except that today I had to undergo all sorts of physical tests. I needed sports shorts and running shoes.

Luckily, the woman in the next room was Becky Cashman, daughter of one of the Tampa Bay team directors. To help me out, she lent me a pair of jean shorts and a black T-shirt with the inscription "Real Men Wear Black." Unfortunately, she didn't have any running shoes, but I was thankful for what she could offer me. It was better than nothing.

When I came out of my room dressed in this get-up, the reporters cracked up: the only girl on the team wearing such a T-shirt! I was shy. I didn't know where to hide. Naturally, they took lots of photos, which just made me feel worse.

I kept worrying about what the guys were going to think: "Who does she think she is? What's she doing here, anyway? It's bad enough she's a girl and should be keeping a low profile, but now she's going to do her fitness tests in short-shorts and sandals!" I was feeling so bad that I felt I had to explain to everyone who crossed my path about my baggage fiasco. I felt the need to justify myself. It just helped me feel better.

The reporters from Quebec gave me encouragement. They kept telling me that it wasn't as bad as all that, that everything would work out, that my equipment would get here soon and not to sweat it. They could see that I felt uneasy, dressed like that.

So that's the way I had to begin the tests.

The first was a urine sample. I couldn't do it. I didn't have to and I wasn't able to. I especially didn't want to drink any water because after this test, we'd be getting on the scales and I didn't want to be one or two pounds heavier. So I ran cold water on my wrists. It's supposed to help. I don't know how long I did that, but it was a good little while and I still only filled a quarter of the container. It was enough for the test, but by now I was totally fed up. When things go badly, they really go badly.

There were all kinds of tests. They weighed and measured us. They checked our teeth, eyes, muscles, bones, heart. They went over us from top to bottom to see if we could survive training camp.

The tests took up a good part of the day, and still my bags hadn't arrived.

The off-ice fitness tests started, and just as I was about to launch into them my baggage finally arrived, and I had the right clothes. We had to do sit-ups, push-ups, skipping, endurance tests. Lots of reporters stayed to watch me, and I could feel that everyone was pulling for me. It helped a lot.

I passed all the tests easily. Even in the sit-ups, I was among the best. I wasn't the weakest on any of the tests. That was encouraging. I knew now I didn't look silly. I came out of the test room filled with confidence. So the camp hadn't started off so badly after all!

When I finally managed to leave the arena, the others had long since left. The only person left was my faithful mother, who had waited for me the whole time. So we went for dinner and a chat, just the two of us.

The next day, we hit the ice.

The camp was simply a series of games during which the eight teams would alternately play each other. The goalies would have the same amount of ice time, the same number of periods. Same chance for everyone. It was up to me to play well and to show them what I could do.

In the first game, Wendell Young played for the first period and I took the net for the second. That was lucky, because it gave me a chance to observe the game, the passes, the speed of play. I was definitely not in the kids' leagues any more. I was struck by the world of difference.

Throughout the first period, I tried to put myself in the place of Wendell and the opposing goalie. I tried to envision myself in net and exactly how I would stop the shots they were now facing. I was actually moving along with them as I sat on the bench, and my heart was pounding as if I were in the game.

After the first period, the team returned to the dressing room. I was fighting a losing battle against a nervousness that I could feel right up into my throat. I could hardly breathe, there were a million butterflies in my stomach, and the skin on my face was on fire. My whole body felt feverish. I tried to concentrate, to visualize the breakaways, the shots, the nice saves.

I was completely lost in my thoughts when someone, an equipment supplier, appeared in front of me asking me to try on a mask. It didn't seem to faze him in the least that he was breaking my concentration. It was obvious he had no idea whatsoever of what this upcoming period of hockey represented to me. But I was lost in the ozone, unable to get upset.

One of the veteran players—I don't know who because I was too far gone to even recognize his voice—said to the guy, "Can't you see she's getting ready to play in net in the next period? Come back after the game. She doesn't need to lose her concentration over a bloody mask!"

Boy, did those words ever sound good! All of a sudden I was aware that one of the players had come to my defense, that he was on my side. What a feeling!

Finally, it was time to head out to the ice for the second period. My period. My legs were shaking. I knew the most important shot would be the first one. I knew I had to stop that one at all costs to feel confident. And that's what happened. All the tension drained out of me as soon as I blocked that first shot.

I have to say that the first shots weren't all that hard. Each player seemed to be shooting with a little smile on his face, as if they were all saying, "We'll show this little lady what real hockey is." But as soon as they saw that I was stopping the pucks, they wiped the smiles from their faces and started shooting for real.

I could clearly see everything that was happening on the ice—all the plays unfolding, all the passing, all the deking. My mind was totally in tune with my body. I was invincible. There were no cracks in the wall.

And I pulled it off! I didn't allow a goal in fifteen shots. When there were only ten seconds left in the period, I let myself believe that a shutout was possible. I told myself, "You did it, Manon. Even if you allow a goal now, you can truly say 'Mission Accomplished.'" And those last ten seconds passed without a goal.

After the game, the coach made us skate. The guys all came up to congratulate me. I could feel they were surprised and proud at the same time. One of them even said, "Some of the guys thought you would let in six or seven goals. You really shut them up. They're going to take you seriously now."

I was walking on air when I went back to my room. I sat down on a chair. I didn't feel a bit tired. The mirror in front of me reflected an image I will never forget: my face was calm, my eyes shone like never before, and I couldn't stop smiling. There seemed to be shimmering white and emerald green lights around me. My aura, I guess.

I felt a pride in myself like never before. This was a professional camp and I hadn't allowed a goal. I still couldn't believe it. Through a half-open door, I caught a glimpse of Phil Esposito, who gave me a nice smile, as if to say, "Way to go! You showed them you could do it." One after the other, the rest of the coaches came up to congratulate me.

The reason I was so pleased to have succeeded so well in this first period was that people are quick to pass judgment, right off the bat. That first period was very significant. But I didn't want to get carried away too quickly—it was only one period in a whole training camp. I wanted to be realistic, but at the same time I was very happy about my successful debut.

After the news conference, I went to the hotel to look for my mom, who'd watched the whole thing from the stands. She was as happy as I was. She never worried about me getting injured in the play, but she was anxious that I might be hurt by the comments if it didn't go well. If it had gone badly for me on the ice, she would have suffered along with me.

She was as proud as if it had been her own victory. I had shown those skeptics that I could guard the net.

Throughout training camp, I had to do interviews, photo sessions, television and radio shows and return dozens of phone calls while the other players were playing golf, having fun and taking it easy. I could never relax, I was running around all over the place. I had expected that when I came to Tampa Bay, though. There was no choice for me but to think, live and breathe hockey twenty-four hours a day. Not a moment's rest.

As soon as the day's training ended, it was a race to get ready for all my other commitments. Luckily, Mom was there.

After showering, there was my hair, make-up and getting dressed, always squeezed into a very short time frame. It was funny to see us sometimes. To help me, Mom would do my hair while I returned my calls. I didn't have a minute to waste. Because the telephone cord wasn't long enough, I would put the phone on the floor between the two beds and, to keep my head still, I would press the numbers with my toes. Two nutballs in action!

While I put on my make-up, she would iron my clothes on the bed. She washed my clothes at night so they would dry overnight, and if they were still damp in the morning, she would blow them dry with the hair dryer. I don't think I could have made it without her there. The only thing she didn't need to do was sing me a lullaby when I finally went to bed at night, because I was asleep before my head hit the pillow.

She didn't see anything of Tampa Bay or Lakeland, where the camp was held. All she saw were the hotel and the arena. Neither of us got any rest except for a few evenings of shopping. That's a weakness we share. It was the only way we could relax.

She was as jittery as I was. She shared everything with me, including the pressure, and there was plenty of that to go around. I had to perform for the media as well as on the ice.

The media pressure was so crazy that Barry Hanrahan, the Lightning's public relations man, started screening calls. It had become hell. Now, no one could call me directly at my hotel room.

The hockey part went well, though. I never had a bad game. Naturally, I gave up a goal or two every game, but I was steady and never had a bad match. At the end of the first week, I had the third-best goals-against average of the eight netminders. With the little experience I had, I could be very happy with that.

After the first week, some of the players were cut, but I didn't get the chop. I would stay on, with five other goalies.

It was also at the end of the first week that my mom had to leave me on my own. She had to return to her job in Quebec. She was indispensable to me, but her boss obviously felt the same way.

During the second week of camp, it was mainly practices and no games. Morning and night. I got in as much ice time as possible, arriving at the arena before everyone else and staying on after they left. I really wanted to learn. There would never be another chance like this. I had to savor every moment, get maximum benefit, waste nothing.

I trained so hard that a thigh muscle rebelled. One morning it decided it didn't want to play hockey any longer. It was fed up. I had to sit out the day's session to rest. I wasn't exactly ecstatic about that. I realize I'm not made of steel, but injuries have always been my worst enemy. I don't want to get hurt. I don't have the right to, either, because the minute I do, I hear comments like: "No surprise, she's a girl."

I only missed one session. The treatments helped a lot and my pride did the rest.

Finally, at the very end of the camp, came the time for the exhibition games with other National Hockey League teams.

The team began to get more and more nervous, because the final player cuts were approaching. The guillotine was hanging over all our heads.

One evening, Phil Esposito came up to me with a big smile and said casually, as if it were no big deal, "If you're feeling good after tomorrow's practice, you'll play net tomorrow night. You're going in for one period." It certainly was a big deal for me. I immediately told Hanrahan to refuse all interviews for me. I wanted absolutely nothing else on my mind. All I wanted was to rest, relax and concentrate on the coming game. And not be bothered.

On the night of the game against the Saint Louis Blues, there was no noise on the bus taking us to the arena. The tension was palpable. Everybody was wondering if he would have a job after the game. I was nervous, too. So far, I had had a good camp and I knew the team directors were happy with me. But what were they expecting of me? What did they have in mind? Were they going to play this game right up to the very end?

I can still see myself entering the arena on September 23, 1992. I can still feel the tension that gripped me as I walked down the corridor to my room. I can remember every single thought that ran through my head as I sat there on the bench in my room alone, staring at my equipment. My armor ...

It hangs there on a nail on the wall, looking for all the world like a spooky giant puppet. Empty, lifeless, waiting to come alive, waiting to be put on, to play a role. The chest-protector, the goalie pads, the well-worn hockey pants that I've been wearing since my Peewee days, the white sweater with a black lightning bolt across the front and a big number 33 on the back. And up above, the black mask with its big face-protector, looking like it's about to bite someone. On the floor, the skates, the gloves, the stick.

Okay, let's do it!

Breathe deeply, Manon. Breathe. Say goodbye to this fear

in the pit of your stomach. Fear? No, Manon, not fear. A little case of nerves, that's all.

Breathe, Manon. Breathe.

These Saint Louis Blues are no big deal. You'll shut them down.

Picture it ... yeah, that's it ... I see him coming at me, the big Blues player, puck on his stick. You can elude my defensemen, try to deke me all you want, pal, but this is the end of the line. He fires the puck! I snag it in my glove! Another Blues player takes the rebound. C'mon, shoot, man! Just try me! I block it again, this time with my leg pad. Yeah, Manon may not be big, but she's mighty quick!

Breathe, Manon. Breathe. You always wanted to play in the big leagues and now you're here. It's your big day. You can't blow this chance. Take advantage of it. Enjoy it.

It's going to go well. It's just another hockey game. The pucks fly and you stop them, just like always. Simple.

Okay, let's get moving! Enough daydreaming. Get dressed, girl. Put on your armor.

This is the key moment of the Tampa Bay Lightning training camp: the game against the Saint Louis Blues.

One by one, the players leave the dressing room and head for the ice for the warmup.

I feel the nervousness in the pit of my stomach and my heart is beating a little faster than usual, but I don't really feel the stress yet. I know I'll be coming back to the dressing room after the warmup and that there will be one more moment of respite before the big game. Before my first period.

The warmup goes well. My teammates boost my confidence, aiming most of their shots at my leg pads. They don't baby me but they don't try to trick me with every shot, either. They don't shoot soft shots. They shoot normally.

They encourage me with their words: "Just play the way you have since the beginning of camp. You'll be great. Don't sweat it."

It's a really good warmup. I feel in control. The crowd is warming up too, clapping and cheering at my every save. The stands are filling up.

The camera flashes are exploding in my face—and the game hasn't even started yet.

It'll be a breeze, Manon. Just stay focused.

And breathe.

Oh, God! The warmup is over already. Back to the dressing room for a few minutes. After that, it's not a joke any more. It's for real.

Breathe, Manon. Breathe.

Not a word is uttered in the Lightning's dressing room. It doesn't get any more tense than this. Everyone is concentrating; everyone wants to play well; everyone wants to make the team. Everybody is playing for their future. Playing for their life, in other words.

All of a sudden, the stress is winning. I'm burning up and my cheeks feel like they're on fire. Surely the others can hear my heart pounding. But no, everyone is listening to their own heart. They're wrapped up in their own thoughts.

Coach Terry Crisp gives his final instructions.

I don my mask.

Breathe, Manon. Breathe.

In the corridor leading to the ice, not a sound. But as we walk toward the rink, the dull buzz of the crowd noise vibrates in our ears. How many people are there out there?

Oh, Mom, I know you're not out there in the crowd. But I know you're thinking about me, at home in front of your television. Send me some good vibes.

The players are introduced and the national anthem is being sung. I'm standing in front of my net, in a trance. I can see the flag clearly ... but who's singing? A man, a woman ... I wouldn't know. I can't hear a thing.

Breathe slowly, Manon.

The anthem is over, because the players take their positions on the ice. The crowd is yelling, but all I hear is a vague background noise.

You're really focused, girl, your concentration is excellent. It's going to go well.

Then the puck is dropped and it seems to me to be whipping about at a ridiculous speed. The passes, the plays, everything seems to be taking place on fast-forward.

What's that? No way! A whistle. Not even thirty seconds into the game and they've called a penalty against us. Now they've got the player advantage right away. Shit!

Okay, the play is started again. Concentrate twice as hard, Manon. No sweat.

There's a player coming at you. Look out! He's going to shoot!

Well done, girl. A good stop and the crowd loves it, too. Listen to the noise.

Now concentrate on the game, Manon. You stopped the first shot and that's always the toughest one. From here on, it'll be like taking candy from a baby.

Whoa, look out, Manon! They're attacking from this side now.

Blocked again, and the crowd roars!

They're coming at me again. Give me a break!

Blocked! Roar! What a great feeling to have the crowd with you.

The penalty is over. That was the longest two minutes of my life. Okay, pay attention! Jeff Brown has a breakaway. Oh, no. Shit. It's in! He shot from the back of the circle and it went in! The puck bounced from one pad to the other before going through my legs. Bing, bang, then right through an impossibly small opening. Shit! What an insult! I could have stopped that shot.

Breathe, Manon. Breathe slowly.

As far as I'm concerned, it's not 1-0, it's still 0-0. Okay, Jeff Brown. Try me again. You won't get two in a row.

Look out! This two-on-one coming down the ice doesn't look good. Dangerous ... dangerous ...

Blocked! Oh, yes, I'm on a roll, now. Bring me those pucks!

Whoops! I never saw it. That'll teach me to call for pucks. I didn't even have time to react. It came from behind the net right off the stick of Brendan Shanahan. Bing, bang, and into the net! It's a drag, but it was a nice goal.

Try me again! The game's not over till it's over.

Time for a breather ... end of the first period: 2-2. *My period is over ...*

It wasn't so bad. Two goals in nine shots—one good one and one lousy one that I should have stopped. It wasn't the performance of the century, not a shutout with fifty shots in the first period, but considering my little experience and all the media pressure, it isn't bad. Not bad at all. I'm very, very pleased.

The crowd is, too, it seems.

Back to the dressing room. Quick, let's get the team together. "Congratulations, Manon, good stuff." "Wow, good girl." "Nice going, kid," "Good job."

Okay, guys. Thanks, but don't lay it on too thick.

Not a word from Crisp. Not a word from Esposito. But their smiles say it all. A mixture of happiness and relief.

My work is finished for the day unless Wendell Young gets hurt. The tension is gone and I can breathe again. I feel really good. I feel too good to feel tired.

It's already time to go back on the ice for the second period warmup. I go, too. I'm skating on air. Am I dreaming, or what?

"Hey, Manon, my coach might not like the idea, but I really have to congratulate you. I can see the look on your face and you've really got a right to be proud of yourself. Way to go!"

Nice words, but it feels even better to hear them from an opponent: Stéphane Quintal, you have no idea how good you make me feel by saying that.

We lose the game 6-4.

Quick. To the shower before the inevitable news conference. There shouldn't be too many reporters there. At least not from Quebec. We tipped them off too late that I was going to play.

The Quebec media weren't there, but the room was full anyway: five television cameras, wall-to-wall photographers, reporters everywhere. It was in that room, because of the questions, that it finally dawned on me that I had just played in a National Hockey League game. Up until that point, I had been trying to act as if it was just an ordinary game in training camp.

There were all kinds of questions, including a real macho one: "Did you break a fingernail?" My blood boiled and I demanded of the reporter, "Would you ask that question of the other goalies?"

I wanted to make him understand that I wanted to be considered like any other player, not as the first woman to play on a pro team. The fact of my being the first was so far from my mind that all this publicity shocked me. I didn't really realize the import of the whole affair.

I'd been given a chance to climb even higher and I was taking it. That was my goal.

That was my dream.

I wasn't good enough to stay in Tampa Bay, but Esposito and Crisp, recognizing my efforts and abilities, decided to send me to the training camp for their farm club, the Atlanta Knights of the International League.

I had surprised them. They hadn't expected so much from me, in light of the little experience I'd had before arriving in camp. For sure, I had to perform well at the Atlanta training camp, but I knew they were interested in keeping me on as the third-string goalie for the Knights. By keeping me in their farm club, they could make me practice every day and watch how much I would develop. They would give me the chance to make up for lost time.

They want to see the difference next year. And they will!

NICOLE RHÉAUME

I tried to stick by Manon during the Tampa Bay training camp. I wouldn't have missed that for anything.

I liked the way the guys from the Lightning treated her. At the start of the camp, for most of them, she was just a gimmick to attract attention to the club. Those she had met earlier in the year for the club's promotions knew her better and knew what to expect of her. They could see her potential.

The guys were very gentlemanly. None of their words or actions were out of line. They thought she was very pretty, but they never tried to date her. They all kept their place—as teammates.

Manon started winning the skeptics over on the day of the physical tests, on the first day of the camp. She surprised even me. I hadn't seen her all summer. She was always gone on promotional tours or trips for her work. She had trained hard during the weeks leading up to the camp and the results were impressive.

She didn't skate as fast as the boys. That's normal, since they are stronger and have longer legs. On the other hand, she kept up with them all the time, doing what they did. She never complained. She was out of breath, sure, but she never doubled over like some of them. She stood up straight.

She is so proud.

She won over the team's last disbelievers during the first practice game. It was a quite a game.

When she stepped out on the ice, all eyes were on her. The media were there with cameras everywhere, flashes and microphones. There were eyes everywhere. There was a lot of pressure on my little girl.

The speed of the shots took my breath away. I knew she wasn't afraid of the puck, but she had to prove that to her teammates.

At times, it was so exciting I couldn't handle what was happening on the ice, especially when there were pileups around the net. Sometimes I couldn't see her anymore. She was under a pile of these big guys six feet tall, 190 pounds. Then, all of a sudden, there she was. I could breathe again.

It's really a strange feeling to see your daughter among all those men.

She was in net for only twenty minutes, but it seemed like an eternity. I watched the shots, the clock, the shots, the clock ... The play was fast—and hard.

Manon met the challenge and held her ground. My baby hadn't let in one goal during her first stint on the ice. She never lost face during the training camp. She maintained everyone's credibility: her own, Tampa Bay scout Jacques Campeau's, and Phil Esposito's.

WENDELL YOUNG, GOALIE, TAMPA BAY LIGHTNING

All I can say as a goalie myself is: Give her time. She's only twenty-one.

How many twenty-one-year-old goalies do you know in the National Hockey League? Not many. Goalies have to be

Every young hockey player dreamed of playing in the Quebec City International Peewee Hockey Tournament. I was the first girl ever to play in it.

"Manon is a performer. When it was time for hockey, she focused totally on that. When it was time to study, her mind was totally on that. There are no halfway efforts with Manon. Because she can concentrate so intensely, she succeeds in everything she undertakes."

– *Nicole Rhéaume*

Companies quickly showed an interest in sponsoring me.

My vampish look. And why not?

On November 26, 1991, because of a lucky combination of circumstances, I played one game with the Trois-Rivières Draveurs. It was the first time a woman had played at the major junior level.

I really like my new life among the jet set. Here I am with Eric Lindros.

During the famous Quebec Major Junior Hockey League game, a powerful shot broke the grill on my mask and my eyebrow was cut. I bled so much that they pulled me in the middle of the third period.

I was invited to the Tampa Bay training camp. My performance was good enough that team owner Phil Esposito decided to keep me. I am now improving my technique with the team's farm club, the Atlanta Knights.

mature and have a lot of experience to be successful.

We were on the same team at training camp in Tampa Bay, the Blues. When I saw her in net during the first game I couldn't believe it. Incredible!

She had good reflexes, moved fast in the net, controlled her territory, and her style wasn't bad at all. She has everything it takes to be a good goalie. She just needs to become physically stronger and improve her cardiovascular system.

With the experience she acquired in Atlanta, she can certainly become a very good goalie. Her small size isn't so important. There have been players just as small who get along quite well: Allan Bester, Mike Richter, Jon Casey, Mike Vernon.

It's up to her. She has to work hard, spend a lot of time training and concentrate on hockey. Fortunately, she seems able to handle the media pressure.

I wouldn't be able to.

8

ATLANTA, HERE I COME

I had taken only a week's worth of clothes with me to Tampa Bay, since I figured I would only make it to the first cut. Not because I was a defeatist, but because I realized I had no experience. I didn't want to start making too many plans. My adventure could well have ended right there.

But life had other plans. The dream would continue.

So, before heading to Atlanta for training camp, I had to return home to Chicoutimi to take care of a few things and repack my suitcases.

There were some big decisions to make this particular weekend. The Knights organization had already let me know that if the camp went well, they would keep me on as third-string goalie.

I had to picture a whole new life.

But what to do with all the proposals for a career in communications that were coming from everywhere? There were several that would have been very attractive to anyone.

And what about my private life? Where would my boyfriend fit in? Would he stay in Chicoutimi or come with me to Atlanta? Would he be drafted by another team in God-knows-where? I was starting to realize that the life of a hockey player demands a lot of sacrifices. I was starting to understand that I was facing the same problems as my male colleagues and that having a private life is no piece of cake.

Throughout the weekend, I remained in close contact with my public relations consultants at NATIONAL in Montreal, looking at my career options and weighing the pros and cons. I wanted to be sure of any decision I made and regret nothing.

There was a news conference in Montreal during this weekend. My public relations adviser, Paul Wilson, warned me that there would be a lot of journalists. But it was still a jolt when he opened the doors to the room.

Even though the room was relatively small, it was packed to the rafters. There were television cameramen, newspaper photographers, reporters everywhere. Everyone was there for me. Everyone was smiling and seemed happy to see me. It was a very warm welcome for my return home to Quebec.

I was incredibly happy and very moved. I could hardly catch my breath. I had an urge to hug all of them, as if it were a family get-together.

Several of the reporters had been skeptical about my Tampa Bay adventure. All they could see was a publicity stunt staged by Phil Esposito. Now, they had changed their minds and weren't embarrassed to say so. They had seen me play and found new respect for me.

Even though I hadn't been fazed by their skepticism, it felt good to witness their new confidence in me.

Obviously, the main question of the day was what I planned to do after the Atlanta training camp. I had to consider the possibility of starting a career in communications, a field that I have been interested in for a long time. I knew that the right thing to do was to weigh the pros and cons coolly and objectively. I had to make the right decision. My logic encouraged me to accept these offers, but in my heart I knew that hockey would win the day. The passion was just too strong. So I confirmed nothing. But in my heart, I knew ...

I was fried when I arrived in Atlanta at one o'clock in the morning. The Tampa Bay camp had been tough—two intensive weeks on the rink, two weeks of media pressure. I'd been so busy I didn't even have time to feel the fatigue.

My two days off in Chicoutimi and Montreal hadn't exactly been restful either, even though they gave me time to decompress a little. The result was that my tiredness finally caught up to me.

On the first day of camp, I could have slept in. I had a good excuse: the late hour of my arrival. I didn't have to go to the meeting, either. But even though I was tired and feeling kind of sick, I went because I didn't want to be the only one missing.

I couldn't do anything on the ice. I was really dead tired. Five minutes before the end of the practice, I had to leave the ice. My face was green and haggard. I would have frightened Frankenstein. I was finished. I have a lot of pride, but I had reached my limit.

The coaches told me to rest in the afternoon and not dress for the evening game. I was to relax in the stands instead. They knew I had just experienced two extremely trying weeks, and that no other player had had such a hard camp. For two weeks, I had been a puppet whose strings were being pulled by everyone. Interviews, photos—everyone wanted a little piece of me.

Other than this one moment of weakness, my camp was like everyone else's. It didn't go badly, but I didn't experience the same sense of satisfaction I'd felt in Tampa Bay. No bad performances, but no extraordinary ones, either. Very, very steady. I gave it my best—everything I could under the circumstances. In fact, I was taking it a little bit easier.

I could afford to be a little bit calm, because the team had already told me they were interested. At the end of the week, they told me officially: "We're keeping you. We're sure we can do something with you."

Whew!

Right away, they gave me a physical fitness regimen. I don't exactly eat nails for breakfast, but I can bench-press a few pounds and I do a few hundred sit-ups a week. I have no plans to compete for the Miss Muscles title—far from it. I work out to improve my cardiovascular system and my muscular endurance. I don't want big muscles, just what I need to be able to stay in the shape a good goalie needs to be in. I try to keep a feminine figure and I have no desire to "bulk up" with extra weight, as boys often do.

They also arranged a meeting with the team nutritionist, Dr. Dan Benardot, who also supervises the diets of the American gymnastics teams. He ordered tests to measure my body density, bone and joint endurance and percentage of body fat. He said I was made to play hockey. My pelvis size is good and I have strong bones that will resist stress fractures. That was the good news! The bad news was that he put me on a diet of less fat and less sugar. Me, who adores desserts! Ow!

Gene Ubriaco, the team trainer, designed an individual workout program, written in French especially for me. In it, he has listed my strong and weak points with suggestions for correcting the latter. He seems sincere when he says he sees possibilities for me in hockey and wants to help me go as far as I can. His program was designed so that the 1992-93 season would be a period for learning technique and for physical and mental preparation. If I put in the necessary effort, I should be able to return in 1993-94 and head into 1995 with hopes of becoming a regular member of the Atlanta Knights and getting more ice time during regular-season games.

If all goes well and I prove myself capable, he expects I could be playing in the National Hockey League in 1995-96.

He believes in me, but I remain a realist. The calibre of play in the NHL is much too high for me now. My goal is to go as far as possible. Where will that be? No idea!

The regular season started right after the camp. I practiced every day. My energy level returned to normal and I started once again to feel the excitement I'd felt in Tampa Bay.

It took a little while for me to sign my contract because of a few complications. Steve Bartlett, my hockey agent, had to meet with Esposito and Knights president Richard Adler to iron out some details. It didn't get in the way of my training, and since I wasn't playing in games, it wasn't important.

One day, David Littman, the first-string goalie, was called up to Tampa Bay because Wendall Young had been injured. I found myself second-string goalie and I had to dress for a game against Cincinnati. All of sudden it became urgent that I sign a contract, and I did so on November 4, 1992, at 3:00 p.m.

I was very proud.

I didn't play against Cincinnati, but I was ready to if called upon.

On any self-respecting team, of course, there is an initiation. You may wonder who initiates who on a team that is in its first year of existence. The veterans—that is, the men who have already played in a professional league—never ask themselves this kind of existential question: they will be the executioners, of course. Thankfully, shaving the heads of new arrivals is no longer in fashion, because I would have locked myself in a room if I'd ended up looking like Sinéad O'Connor. It was all very civilized, as it turned out, and we all laughed like idiots.

The initiation began during a trip to Salt Lake City during the Thanksgiving weekend. We were in the hotel dining room after a game. The veterans had arranged the tables so that the new recruits were seated with their backs to the center of the room, so we weren't able to see too clearly what assorted tricks were being cooked up.

Throughout the meal, the recruits had to perform imitations, of the coach or a singer, or whatever. When my name was pulled from the hat, I had to do the duck dance. I was embarrassed, red like a tomato. But during an evening like that, everyone laughs at everyone. So I started flapping my wings and serenading them. It was beautiful.

Seated at my table were Daniel Vincelette and Jason Lafrenière. They had given me a bit of a warning about the evening and the tricks that would be played on the new recruits.

One of the favorite high jinks is mashed potatoes on the shoes. One of the veterans secretly crawls around under the tables putting mashed potatoes on the shoes of the new players. Ha, ha! I had sworn that they wouldn't get me. But no! Suddenly there was a clinking of forks on glasses. I saw nothing and no one. But I looked down at my shoes and ... Yes! I had been the first to get the potato treatment. Very, very funny ...

The new players were on their guard but the veterans went to great lengths to divert their attention. They were always had, one way or another. Very cunning, these guys. Sometimes even a bit vicious.

One of the veterans asked Christian Campeau to go put mashed potatoes on the shoes of one of his buddies. In return, he was assured that his name would be removed from the hat and he wouldn't have to sing. Happy, he slid under the table, slithered over to his victim, and at the moment when he was about to commit the dirty deed, Daniel Vincelette blew his cover, screaming loudly, "Hey, Christian Campeau is under the table. What are you doing there? You're caught, pal!"

He came out from under the table fast, red as a beet. Obviously, he had to sing his little song anyway.

The initiation continued a few days later in Atlanta.

This time, it was in a restaurant. I had arrived late because of a promotional event I had been doing in Montreal. That netted me a fifty-dollar fine. By the time I arrived, everybody was feeling no pain.

They quickly decided to get me in tune with the party. Normally, I don't drink at all. I don't like alcohol or wine. But that night, I had to partake. First, someone offered me a glass of wine. Then came the shooters. And not in shot glasses. Big ones, in what looked like wine glasses.

I had no idea what kind of drinks I was being handed, but like everyone, I drank them. The B-52s weren't too bad, but there was also tequila and Tabasco sauce. Yech! Disgusting.

After a few drinks, we played pool. I was really bad. I had to shoot two or three times just to hit the ball. Everyone had a good laugh.

Around two in the morning, the team party started to break up. Only a few invincible Quebecers remained at the table. So we all headed for the apartment that Daniel Vincelette and Jean Blouin were sharing.

There, the party continued, with drinking and laughing until the wee hours. Not being in the habit of drinking, I started feeling dizzy at one point. I went into the bathroom to splash some cold water on my face. I decided to sit down for a few minutes to regain my balance, but I fell fast asleep on the spot. After a little while, the guys, who were beginning to get a little worried about my absence, started calling my name and beating on the bathroom door. No answer. Finally, Blouin took a chance and opened the door, only to find me sitting precariously balanced, about to bang my head on the bathtub. They put me on the couch and the party ended there.

I wasn't sick but I had a real hangover the next morning! Everything was spinning, my legs were rubbery, and my head wanted to explode. I won't be drinking again too soon, I guarantee you.

There was a practice scheduled for 10:30 a.m., and so I had to act as if there was nothing wrong and go do my job. It was the first time ever that I didn't feel like playing. Horrible booze!

Blissfully unaware that we had held our initiation the evening before, Gene Ubriaco pushed us harder than he ever had before, including end-to-end skating drills that went on forever. When I say time passed slowly, I mean it dragged!

Strangely, I felt better after practice, having sweated the alcohol out of my system, I guess. It's at times like that that the benefits of physical exercise are felt.

And so my little organized life got back on track: sleep, practice, promotional activities, healthy eating and drinking.

Then one fine day, December 13, I was given the opportunity to really "break the ice."

We were playing at home against the Salt Lake City Golden Eagles. Ubriaco had advised me that I would be playing the first five minutes of the second period. He wanted to give me a bit of ice time and to experience playing in a game.

It was 0-0 after the first period. I was very nervous and feeling more pressure than usual when I skated onto the ice. It wasn't my game and I hadn't warmed up. I was cold, very cold. But I told myself: "I'd better get used to it. I'm eventually going to find myself in this situation as second-string goalie. You never know when the other goaltender will be hurt, and you have to be ready to jump in at any moment. When the coach gives you the signal, you go. No questions asked. So let's go, Manon. It'll be good experience, at any rate." All this was going through my head as I skated onto the ice.

I tried my best, but I let in a goal. I was about twelve feet out of my net to clear the puck. I shot it well but unfortunately it hit a rapidly approaching Todd Gillingham on the shoulder. He skated around me and shot into the empty net. I was disappointed. I had wanted to do better. One goal in four shots ... Really!

A little later in the season, on April 10, 1993, I was given a chance to play an entire game against the Cincinnati Cyclones. Our team's position in the regular-season standings was already assured: the Knights were in first place, so Coach Ubriaco was taking no risk by letting me play. If we lost, the consequences would not be dramatic.

Once again, this provoked a media uproar. The reporters had been asking for me for a long time. They wanted to see what I could do after a few months of training. They wanted to see for themselves if I really deserved to play with the pros in the International League.

That night, there were reporters from Montreal, Quebec City and from all over Canada and the United States. The arena at the Omni Center was filled to capacity with 15,000 fans. There was a thunderous roar from the stands and I could feel that the Knights fans were behind me. Even my parents were there to encourage me.

I fought like the devil and my teammates backed me up, but I made mistakes and had a bit of bad luck. I allowed six goals in thirty-three shots and two more were scored on an empty net. We lost 8-6.

Ubriaco seemed happy with my performance, telling me I had done my job. When I'd arrived in Atlanta a few months earlier, it had been clearly written in my contract that the first year would be a learning experience, that I would practice and that I would not necessarily play in any games.

I am there to learn, and the practices are long. I make it a habit and a point of honor to be the first on the ice and the last off. I have a lot to learn and I'm not afraid of hard work.

I already feel stronger and faster. My reflexes feel sharper.

I would be curious to know how well I would have done at the Tampa Bay camp if I had been in this kind of shape back then. Well, hindsight is always 20-20, and I'll only know more next year.

Until then, I do what I'm told to do. I sometimes travel with the team when we go on the road, so I'm getting to see the United States: Salt Lake City, Cleveland, Cincinnati, San Diego, Phoenix, etc. I like traveling, and my geography, always my weakest subject in school, is improving.

Traveling with the guys is important for me because it helps me feel part of the group. I can't do much for the team when I'm sitting in the stands, but I send them positive vibes—better than nothing. And I also use the time to do some mental practicing.

When I watch the game, I see myself in the goalie's place. I see myself in net and I stop the pucks. It's stronger than me. I'm in the stands moving and stretching to catch a shot. I'd really like to be in there helping. I'd really like to be on the ice.

GENE UBRIACO, COACH, ATLANTA KNIGHTS

If there's one thing I can't stand, it's hearing that someone can't do something without being given a break.

Everybody told me that at five-foot eight I was too small to play in the National Hockey League. Right! I did it anyway. I played for Pittsburgh, Chicago and Oakland.

I volunteer during my summer holidays to help a hockey team of hearing-impaired kids, and I've often heard: "Those kids can't play hockey because they're deaf." But this training program has been around for close to twenty years. These kids can make it on their own.

It's the same thing for Manon Rhéaume. Lots of people say she can't play in a professional league because she's a woman. I can't buy that prejudice.

My first reaction when Phil Esposito talked about drafting her was this: "Let's see what she can do and decide after that."

I watched her for two weeks at the Tampa Bay camp and I saw that she had the right stuff to be a good goalie. What worried me was whether she could handle the pressure. But when I saw her in net during an exhibition game against the Saint Louis Blues, I decided right away to take her on our team. She was in full control of her emotions and her faculties. You don't learn how to react to pressure; you either have it or you don't.

I tailored a training program for her to follow to the letter. If she sticks to it, she can't help but improve.

During the first year, she had to make up for lost time. She had never been able to play more than twice a week. With us, she practices every day on the ice. She also works out in a fitness center, which she had never had the chance to do before. Within a few months, you could already see a clear improvement.

She is much stronger, but she's not quite ready yet to play. She needs more experience. I let her play twice in the first year of her contract so people could see that she can mind the net, so they would look at her as a goalie and not just as a publicity stunt.

Manon is a goalie. When she talks about goaltending technique, she talks like a goalie. She is strong-willed—a goalie's mentality. And she's built like a goalie—just smaller.

For the moment, I have two goalies better than she is. She certainly won't take their place. Manon is still our third "man," and on three or four occasions she has been our backup goalie on the bench when one of the other two has been called up to Tampa Bay. If there had been an injury or poor performance, she would have had to go in.

When we feel she is ready, we will have her playing on a regular basis. Next year, if everything goes well, she should play in fifteen or so games to get some experience. The following year, she'll be playing even more.

I've heard some strong criticisms of her, mainly from Canada. The people who judge her don't know what they're talking about. They are being unnecessarily cruel. If it were only a publicity stunt, it would have ended a long time ago. I don't want to hear any more of that crap.

She takes practice very seriously. She's the first on the ice and stays afterwards to work with me and the other new recruits. She sticks with the regimen and that's all I ask of her.

She has blended in with the group, and nobody even notices any more that she's a woman. I talk to her like I would to any other player. If I had to bring her into line, she would get the same speech as the others. That's the way it has to be. She wants to play hockey? Well, that's how it works.

The fact that she is a woman changes nothing in the way I coach the team. The only thing that worries me is not knowing how she'll react if she's hurt. I know she already got her face cut and that she's taken some heavy hits, but I don't think she's ever really suffered.

I'm sure I'm worrying for nothing. A woman I know reassured me: "Don't worry. Women can take more pain than men." You know, I've never heard her complain. The guys, on the other hand, never stop whining.

One day I forced them to train really hard. I thought the players had been taking it easy for some time and I wanted to give them a shock. It worked. They complained and swore and were grumpy. Just like men, eh?

For her part, she did the routines with just as much effort but there was never a flicker of emotion on her face. She suffered in complete silence.

I found out afterwards that, the night before, there had been an initiation for the new recruits. They had a lot of alcohol in their blood and their legs were a bit wobbly on the ice. I couldn't have picked a better time to sock it to them if I had wanted to!

Manon is very determined, and that's why I want to help her. It will be a great day when she plays a full game.

The day she signed her contract with us, I gave her a cigar to show that she was a full member of the group. The next day she gave me a note that said, "Thanks for believing in me."

I'm keeping that card forever.

9

ALL ALONE IN THE BIG CITY

Making the jump from the little town of Lac Beauport to a city like Trois-Rivières wasn't too difficult. It didn't change my life too much. But jumping from Trois-Rivières to Atlanta was something else entirely. It was nothing less than culture shock.

The first and certainly not least important aspect of my culture shock was the language problem. Like all young Quebecers, I learned my English in school, but I never spoke it. My community was 100 percent French-speaking, and I practically never had an occasion to speak English, except on the rare occasion when a tourist would approach me asking for directions to the Château Frontenac.

Today, after less than a year in Atlanta, my English is greatly improved. I understand everything that is being said and have no difficulty making myself understood. I plan to take courses to improve it even more.

Another aspect of the culture shock was the size of the city and the number of people.

I have always been a little afraid of large cities, including Montreal. I don't really know why. Fear of the unknown, perhaps. We always tend to think that other people are very different from us, and we imagine all sorts of dangers, repeating big-bad-wolf stories when the reality is usually nowhere near as bad as all that. You just have to get to know a city, its neighborhoods, its restaurants, its stores, its people. It can be done, but you have to take the time to visit the city and to really meet its people.

Take the time! That's easy to say!

My life in Atlanta is very different. It's hectic—breathtakingly so. Luckily, I'm young and healthy, or I wouldn't last long.

A little while back, a reporter from Montreal came to Atlanta to do a major article on my life there. For a week, she followed me everywhere except onto the ice. I left her in the dust. She was totally bushed. She couldn't believe everything I did in a day. The only times she could interview me were in the car driving between home and the Omni Center, where we play, or between the Park Air rink where we practice and the fitness center where I work out, or in the evenings when we ate supper in a restaurant.

Between practices and promotional commitments, I don't have a free moment, except during the evening when I take an hour break to call my family and friends. Even then, it's fortunate I have a cordless telephone because I do a thousand things while I'm talking: wash and fold the laundry, load the dishwasher, organize the apartment a bit so that the cleaning lady won't be too discouraged the next time she visits, sign hockey cards on the table, open my mail, prepare meals.

When it's finally time for dinner, I sit in front of the television watching a rented video, one of my only diversions. I sit there like a couch potato, too tired to move. Around nine o'clock I usually manage to drag myself to bed and hide under the covers. Exciting life, eh?

It has to be that way, because otherwise I wouldn't be able to handle the pace. I need at least ten hours of sleep to recover from my day. So I don't go out much with the guys on the team after the games. They invite me to go to movies or restaurants with them, but I usually decline because I'm no good to anyone after nine o'clock.

When you look at all the promotional activities, radio and television interviews, the filming of ads, meetings with company presidents who want me to endorse their products or with salespeople who want me to wear their equipment or use their sticks, it's unbelievable how many people I meet in a day. But in the end I'm totally alone. Alone in a crowd.

I have made only one girlfriend in my time in Atlanta, but she's a good one: Hilary. I met her at a sports card show, right after I arrived in Atlanta. She was working for the Classic company, with whom I do business. She was the first woman I'd been able to talk to in weeks, because the wives and girlfriends of the other players had not yet arrived in town. I was living in a men's world. That was nothing new, but it sure did me good to speak to another woman about female interests.

We hit it off right away. We went out together a few times and she introduced me to some of the city. On the first evening we went out for supper together, I fell in love with the area where she lives. Now we're neighbors.

At that time, I had been looking for a place to live for quite a while. The neighborhood where most of the guys on the team live isn't bad, but I preferred Hilary's area. I liked the apartment design better: more open, with a large living room and big windows. The neighborhood also seemed much safer: automatic gates for the parking area, an access code for the main and apartment doors. This is something that shouldn't be taken too lightly in a large city like Atlanta. A couple of other small details tipped the scales in favor of Hilary's apartment block: a cleaning service and free take-out breakfasts! This is really great when you're pressed for time in the morning. You just grab a muffin and a juice on the run and eat in the car. No time lost.

Losing time is my worst phobia. I detest it. I am the most impatient girl in town. When I'm driving on the highway, I have to fly. People who cruise in the left-hand lane without passing drive me crazy. Don't even talk about traffic jams. I explode! Sitting waiting in a parking lot, while the woman in the car whose space I'm about to take applies her makeup, exasperates me. Waiting in line at the grocery store to pay for something is a nightmare. I have no time to lose, it's so precious. I just have too many things to do.

If I stay inactive for ten minutes, I'm bored. I cannot just sit quietly somewhere and do nothing. My mother pointed this out to me during one of my visits to Lac Beauport. I have to correct this. I have to learn how to take a breather once in a while. But it will come with time. For now, that's just the way it is. I'll take it easier a little later in my life, in a few years when I can't play hockey any longer. But until then, I live life at double-time, all the time.

A typical day for me starts at 7:00 a.m. I eat a light breakfast: fruit juice, natural, non-fat raisin bread, sometimes wheat germ. Although the free breakfasts in my building helped to attract me there, I no longer eat them because of their high fat and sugar content.

I have, in fact, radically altered my eating habits since coming to Atlanta. I try to eliminate all fat from my diet. Thanks to the advice of Dr. Benardot, I have been able to considerably reduce my percentage of body fat and increase my muscle mass, while also losing weight. I have never felt better in my life.

Besides fueling my body with healthy food, I also follow the advice of my main guru, Daniel Bouchard, the former Quebec Nordiques netminder who is now the team's goaltending coach. Daniel has been my idol since I was a little girl. I have always admired him. As luck would have it, I am goaltending in a city where Daniel himself played when the Flames were based in Atlanta, quite some time ago.

We were sitting beside each other in the Omni Center stands one evening when he had come to watch the Knights play. He pointed out all sorts of little details about the goalies' style of play. He gave me a lot of excellent advice, and one of the things he told me about was the importance of feeding my mind.

"Every morning," he explained, "you feed your body to give it energy, so that it can make it through the day. That's fine, but did you think about feeding your mind? You must, absolutely, or you will lose your equilibrium. Your mind has to think fast, to make quick decisions. It must be sharp, alert.

"You should read every morning. Not much. Only a few pages. Books that contain positive thoughts, books that provide lessons on life that are easy to understand."

I took this advice to heart, and every morning I read a little bit of *Osez rêver* (*Dare to Dream*) by Florence Littauer. These are stories about people who have succeeded in life because they want to, because they have decided that they will succeed. They visualize what they want and they go after it. Ever since I began doing this in the morning, I've felt better mentally. My morale and my ability to concentrate have improved.

Daniel is a real gentleman. At the beginning of the season, he offered to let me live with his family. He works in Quebec City with the Nordiques, but his family is still living in a very pretty house in Atlanta. It was tempting, but I gratefully declined, mainly because of my rather special way of life, with an unusual schedule and a very strict diet. I can't impose all of that on another family.

So, after nourishing my mind with positive thoughts, I hop into my car and make a dash for the rink.

Generally, I arrive at the rink at about 9:30 a.m. By the time I check things out a little bit, discuss a few problems with Gene Ubriaco or his assistant, check the promotional agenda with Greg Dewalt, the team's public relations man, it's already time to dress for practice.

As I mentioned, I make it a principle to be the first on the ice. I have so much catching up to do on my teammates that I can't lose a minute. On the contrary, if I could, if it were humanly possible, I would stay twice as long as they do. As third-string goalie, I have less ice time during the practices and fewer shots. So I stay longer, along with the other newcomers, who shoot and shoot and shoot while I save, save, save ...

After two and a half hours of practice, we head for the showers. Does it feel good! I would love to linger under the hot water, massaging my sore muscles, but I don't have the time. I'm always thinking about my schedule.

While I'm walking to my car, I munch on a snack to tide me over until my next meal. Something healthy, naturally. "Organic swill" as a friend once jokingly described it.

I head for the fitness center, where I find Gerry Hall, who is responsible for keeping the team in shape. For an hour and a half, I work on improving my cardiovascular system and my muscular endurance. The fitness center employees are really nice. They push me hard, but good humor helps the time pass quickly.

My workout finished, I put on something warm over my sweaty clothes and head home to shower. I prefer it because it's easier that way—no need to drag around all my stuff: shampoo, towels, clean clothes, a curling iron to take the curl out of my hair.

Yes, I'll let you in on a secret! My straight, sleek hair isn't natural. My hair is curly. It's a mess—curly in some places, straight in others. It sticks out all over the place. So when I do my hair, I have to take the curl out first. It takes a long, long time, and naturally it bugs me—me, who has no time to waste! Sometimes I'll take shortcuts, but I always regret it, because my hair has a mind of its own.

Getting myself prepared for a promotional activity or an interview is a long ordeal. And since I usually have one or another right after a practice, my bathroom always looks like a bomb exploded. Pity the poor cleaning lady!

Since Atlanta is very spread out and I often have two promotional events to attend the same afternoon, I'm always on the highway.

My life is a real marathon, but I love my work.

*   *   *

I never really wanted to be a media star. I didn't ask for all the attention.

At first, reporters thought it was "cute" when I was played in net during the Quebec City International Peewee Hockey Tournament in 1984. A little girl out there with all those little boys was something of a curiosity. The Quebec City reporters continued to follow my career, but it was only a local story.

The real trouble started when the media pounced on the news of my one period in goal for the Trois-Rivières Draveurs of the Quebec Major Junior Hockey League on November 26, 1991. All of a sudden there were reporters from all over North America calling for interviews. All I did was answer their questions.

It was a hoot for them. I was fresh meat for the media mill, something different for their readers or viewers, a new phenomenon to be explored.

It was news for them, but not for me.

All I could do was answer the questions, but I quickly started feeling that things were getting out of control. I was starting to worry. That was when we turned to NATIONAL Public Relations for help. I can still see us in the office of Executive Vice-President Daniel Lamarre. We laid out our problem and asked him to take us on as a client. He didn't seem too enthused.

Later I learned that he was sure my parents wanted to exploit the situation to make money with the story.

After more conversations, his thinking changed. He realized that my parents wanted to protect me and that they needed help. He could see that I wasn't making this up, that I was serious, and that, while I loved hockey, we had to keep it within some reasonable perspective.

At the start, we had agreed to every single request for an interview. I don't think there was a single radio or TV station, not one Quebec newspaper, that hadn't interviewed me. It was crazy. Even back then, I had almost no time for myself.

We had to make some choices.

There was even a request from *Playboy* magazine. They were offering to pay up to $40,000 for an interview and photo shoot, an enticing amount of money. But money can't replace personal pride. People were telling me that it wouldn't be that bad, that this was a modern world, that I should take advantage of the offer.

No way! I simply was not interested. The decision was an easy one for me, and NATIONAL did the rest.

After the *Playboy* offer, there was the invitation to the Tampa Bay training camp, which attracted more media interest. It was really getting out of hand. Requests were coming in from the United States, Europe, North Africa and Japan. This situation was simply not going to disappear.

I remember, in particular, an interview in Montreal with Réjean Tremblay of *La Presse*. We both had a good laugh.

As he was interviewing me about my selection for the Atlanta Knights, he said, "You know, Manon, if I'd written something like this five years ago in 'Lance et compte,' everybody would have thought I was nuts."

"Réjean, don't you remember that five years ago there was a girl from the Quebec City region who called you with exactly that idea?"

"Yeah ... maybe."

"Well, that girl was me."

"You're kidding! I should have jumped at the chance. Everybody would have said I was a genius."

A little later, an appearance on "Late Night With David Letterman" made me well known in the United States. That had a very big effect on my popularity. In fact, a survey about Quebec's favorite athletes, done by Léger et Léger in 1992, ranked me fourth after Sylvie Bernier, Myriam Bédard and Sylvie Daigle. *USA Today* had me in thirteenth spot, just ahead of Mario Lemieux, in December of 1992. *Time* magazine noted that I was the first woman to play professionally and had me as the seventh wonder of the sports world that year!

Right from the start, the media were split on whether I could succeed. There were, understandably, some skeptics. My presence bothers some people because it upsets their values, and that's normal. I respect their opinions. But I ask them to respect mine, too. Just let me try and we'll see what happens.

Now, the skeptics are having second thoughts.

It all started the day when Patrick Roy agreed to give me some tips during a Canadiens practice at the Montreal Forum.

At the start, the players gave me some easy shots. Then they saw I was blocking them all. The shooting got harder, and I kept on stopping them. Then they started with their slapshots and ... let's just say they were surprised. So were the reporters who were watching from the stands.

But I know there are still lots of skeptics. They make no bones about it, and sometimes they're even a bit nasty. I try not to let that bother me, but I can't shut out all the comments. Sometimes it hurts. I'm not a block of wood. I do have emotions. But this is all part of the game. With time, I'll develop a thicker skin—or stop reading the papers, like most of the players.

I realize that I'm not National Hockey League calibre right now. I'm in Atlanta to learn. I have a three-year contract to develop, and that's exactly what I'm doing. We'll see what happens at the end of the contract. If it's benefiting Phil Esposito, too, so much the better. I'm learning and having a terrific experience. It's a fair deal.

The media can chase me all they want. They can talk about me as often and in whatever way they want. Personally, I know where I'm coming from and where I'm heading. I'm not too sure exactly where it will all end up, but at least I'll have followed my passion.

RÉJEAN HOULE, FORMER MONTREAL CANADIENS PLAYER

I had a chance to meet Manon when she was passing through Montreal, between the Tampa Bay and Atlanta camps.

I had crossed paths with her a few times before but we had never really spoken. My friend Daniel Lamarre of NATIONAL Public Relations suggested we have supper. He wanted me to share with Manon, and her then boyfriend, Claude Poirier, my experiences as a former professional hockey player. He wanted me to talk about that milieu, about the ups and downs of a life in sports, pitfalls to watch out for, how to react to certain situations.

It was a very pleasant experience. I saw a determined young woman, with a lot of will power and perseverance. She seemed very confident and quite bright.

She's very much aware of what's happening to her. She knows very well that she's getting much more media attention than any other ordinary junior player. Because she's the first woman to enter professional hockey, all the cameras are pointed at her. I think she's level-headed enough to keep on acting normally, despite it all.

The route she has to take for now is to improve. Day after day. To become stronger, both physically and technically. She has to prove that she really wants to be a hockey player, that it's not just a passing fancy. Judging from her attitude, it seems to me that she is serious.

To break in, she will have to make a major effort. She has to make her own way, create her own place. She'll have to work to get there. Above all, she mustn't think that because she's a woman she will get special treatment. On the contrary, she always has to be on the same footing as her male team-mates. She has to fit in with the players, be part of the group. Normally, in a group of guys, there are a few who are not polite, a bit out of line, but the vast majority behave. She will get their respect quickly, I'm sure.

Obviously, it's new and different to have a woman at the professional level, and that can hurt some male egos. The fact that she spent very little time in the juniors has drawn some smart cracks. Nobody likes to see someone with less experience go to the head of the line. That's because it's a very competitive milieu, not necessarily because she's a woman. When I played left wing for the Canadiens, I can assure you that I didn't like to see anyone overtake me.

She has to work very, very hard. Double-time. With some hard practice, everyone can improve. It's all up to her. She has to show everyone who thinks she cut into the line that she's got the talent and the desire to be a goalie.

She also has to keep in mind that players can be put on a pedestal very quickly by the public but they can fall off just as quickly if they don't live up to their billing. A player can be totally forgotten, and that hurts. The fans demand a lot from professional athletes, particularly with today's salaries.

I reminded Manon and Claude—and I'm sure they know it—that you can't kid yourself. Many are called but few are chosen. Only 250 players are picked in the major junior draft. Of those, 20 or maybe 25 will make the National Hockey League. That's not many. You have to face that reality.

But mainly, I told her that the important thing is to do what she wants to do. To go to the limit of her ambitions. To stick to it and put a lot of effort into improving. To do her time in the minors, like any other player, before aspiring to go higher. To patiently go through all the steps, one by one.

Time will tell whether she has what it takes to move into the NHL. Let's give her a chance.

Manon, you make your own luck. You're the only one who can do it, and nobody else. Even if you have all the media behind you, if you don't stop the pucks, that's it.

That's the only thing they pay you to do: stop the puck.

10

THE UPS AND DOWNS
OF A DIVA

I get along really well with the guys on the team. I feel accepted and respected by them, on the ice and off.

They tease me a lot but it's okay, because I kind of feel like I'm with my brothers. It's never done in a mean-spirited way and we always have a good laugh. Anyway, if they didn't razz me I'd feel rejected, because they never stop bickering amongst themselves.

I must admit that I mainly hang around with the French-speaking guys on the team. Obviously, it's the language affinity. I don't have problems any more with English, but it was another story at the start. I really had to concentrate on what was being said all around me and it literally gave me a headache. So, when it came time for fun and relaxation, I naturally gravitated toward the French-speakers: Daniel Vincelette, Jean Blouin, Christian Campeau, Éric Dubois, Martin Simard, Jean-Claude Bergeron.

In Atlanta, I'm really a world away from my home. There's no question of escaping for a weekend. Sure, there's the telephone, but it's not the same.

I sometimes find it very hard to go back to my apartment alone. There's always lots to do—hockey cards to sign, letters to answer and phone calls to return—but sometimes talking to my stuffed animals isn't enough.

I had to break up with my boyfriend, Claude.

He had come to live with me in Atlanta at the beginning of the season. He was hoping to play in the American League and was awaiting news from various clubs.

While I was out practicing and doing my promotional activities, he was waiting for me in the apartment. No team called. He found the days long and boring. In time, we grew apart, and he returned to Montreal to live with his parents.

It's hard enough to be the partner of a pro hockey player. But when both members of the couple are hoping to make it in the big leagues, there's quarreling, stubbornness and unhappiness.

I guess my most painful moment since coming to Atlanta was last Christmas Day.

I celebrated the traditional French-Canadian réveillon on Christmas Eve at my parents' home, but then I had to hop on a plane for Atlanta early the next morning. I was tired because Paul Wilson, my public relations adviser, had kept me on the run earlier with all sorts of promotional activities in Montreal. I had had only a few hours to rest and see my family.

When I arrived at my apartment, it was dead. Not a light or a sound. And no one there, obviously. You can't imagine how depressed I felt. I could hear the sounds of celebration in the neighboring apartments—laughter, shouts of joy, the noises of happy family moments. At my place, silence and darkness. An empty fridge. No, wait! A can of Diet Coke. O joy, happiness!

O misery!

I went to bed right away just to make the time pass more quickly.

The next day, life returned to normal. Practice at 10:30 a.m. and everyone had to be there, no matter what shape they were in. Parties were not allowed to upset the team's schedule; even less so its performances.

A few days later, something very unpleasant occurred. I call it my night of horror.

I had just spent an evening like any other. While my supper was heating up, I returned calls; while I watched my video, I signed hockey cards.

Around 9:00 p.m., just as I had turned off the bedside light, I heard the elevator doors open. Normally, I wouldn't even pay any attention, but that night ... for some reason, my sixth sense alerted me to something. Maybe I wouldn't have been so edgy about it if I had not, a few days earlier, received some strange phone calls: when I picked up the phone, the caller hung up.

I knew the only neighbors on my floor were away—probably for the Christmas holidays—because telephone directories delivered to their doors had gone untouched for several days.

Then the noise of slow, careful footsteps made me sit bolt upright in bed. My heart was beating so hard I thought it would jump out of my mouth. I felt a cold sweat coming on.

133

My sixth sense hadn't failed me. I can still picture what happened in the next few moments as if it happened only a few hours ago.

The footsteps slowly approached my door. They hesitated. Passed by. Returned. Stopped. Someone tried to open my door, fiddle with the lock. The sound was so slight I could barely hear it. But it wasn't a dream, I was sure of that.

I heard the handle turn, but the door didn't open. Then, again, the noise of the lock and the door shaking.

I was trembling all over. Since I can't see my front door from my bedroom, I would have had to get up, but I couldn't. I was paralyzed with terror.

I finally managed to release my death grip on my blankets and grabbed the portable phone beside the bed. I dialed the number without thinking, as the sweat rolled down my face. I could hear the door being shaken harder and harder.

"Yes, hello?" It was my father's voice.

The words didn't want to come out, my throat was so tight. Finally, out croaked a husky "Pierre," barely audible. It was a true nightmare, but I knew I wasn't dreaming.

My father recognized me anyway and started yelling my name. That jolted me out of my state of shock.

"Daddy, there's someone trying to get into my apartment. He's shaking my door. I'm afraid! I'm afraid!"

"Is he beating on the door? Is he trying to break it down?"

"No, he's not beating on it, but he's shaking it. Daddy, I'm afraid! He's making a terrible noise now."

"Hang up right now and call the police. Right now! Do you hear me? Right now!"

Manon, it's obvious you should call the police. What do

you expect your dad to do for you a thousand miles away? Get a grip!

"Hello, police? Come to my place, right away. Someone's trying to get in. He's trying to break the lock on my door. Hurry! I'm afraid."

"Calm down, we're sending a car right away."

"Don't hang up, miss. Don't leave me alone."

"Do you still hear the noise?"

"No. The handle isn't turning any more. He isn't beating on the door any more. But he's still there. I'm sure of it. Don't hang up! Don't hang up!"

"Don't worry, I won't hang up. I'll wait with you till the police get there. Calm down. Maybe a neighbor has the wrong door."

"No, all my neighbors are all gone for the holidays."

"Maybe it's someone who lives on another floor. You know how people drink at Christmas, press on the wrong elevator button, get off at the wrong floor without even being aware of it."

"I don't know! All I know is I'm afraid. He had to hear me talking to you and he stopped. Don't hang up or he'll start again."

"Calm down. The officers are already at the main door. But they can't get in. You have to push the buzzer on the phone to let them in."

"I can't, I'll have to hang up. I don't want to. I want to keep talking to you."

"Listen! You have to hang up or else go down and let them in. I'm sure the guy is gone. He heard you call the police and he must have heard the siren, too. I'm staying in contact with you, I'm not going to hang up. Open the door a crack and check the hall before you go down."

"No. I'm too afraid!"

"Open the door and check. There's no danger any more. Go!"

"Okay. Don't leave me. God, I'm scared. I think I'm going to faint. There's no one in the hall."

"Good, go to the elevator."

"Okay, but what if he's in the elevator?"

"No, no, he won't be there. Go."

"The elevator's coming. I really think I'm going to pass out ... Okay, there's no one in there ... I'm going down, but what if he's downstairs near the exit door?"

"There's no danger. The police are there."

"So you say! I'm coming to the lobby ... the elevator door is opening ... Aaaaaaiiiiee!" I saw someone in the lobby—I didn't realize at first that it was a police officer!

"Take it easy, miss! There's no more danger. Police. We're here, miss, take it easy."

"The police ... I thought you were the maniac. Hey, why are you pointing your guns at me? And how did you get in here anyway, with the doors closed?"

"Someone else opened them for us. Let's go up to your place. Calm down. It's over. It's over."

They checked the place inside out and there was no more maniac around. The police bade me goodnight, suggesting that I lock my door well (as if I wouldn't have thought of that myself), and told me to call them if I ever needed a bodyguard.

What a time to pour on the charm! That was just about the last thing I needed!

All this time, my poor parents were beside themselves with worry at home, anxiously waiting for me to call back. They were so relieved to hear my voice. I was in one piece, but not in the greatest condition. They did everything they could to build up my morale, but it was a losing battle in the state I was in. They suggested I call up one of my teammates and that I spend the rest of the night somewhere else, not stay alone.

I took their advice and called Daniel Vincelette and Jean Blouin, who share an apartment. Then I got back on the phone to my parents so I could talk to someone while I waited.

Since Dan's Volkswagen wasn't running, Jean came to get me. When he arrived at the cast-iron gate at my building, he dialed my apartment. A male voice responded that there was no Manon there.

"What do you mean, no Manon? You just wait till I get there, you creep!"

He was sure that my maniac had returned and was in my apartment. He left his car right there, managed to open the building doors, dashed up to my apartment and smashed open my door.

"AAAAIIIEEEE!"

For the second time in one evening, I thought I would die. He had dialed the wrong apartment and spoken to who-knows-who!

You should have seen his face when he stormed in. And then, when he realized everything was all right: "Yo, it's me!"

What a commotion!

Safe and sound at my teammates' place, just about back to normal, I told Dan what had happened. The hypothesis of the confused neighbor came up again, but I was convinced.

"No way, he has a key to my place, and it's not the first time he's come in, that guy. He came earlier in the day. He didn't take anything or move anything but he put a lime and some lemons in my suitcase. I didn't have time to completely unpack it when we came back from Cleveland this morning. This is a nut case we're talking about here. He came in my room, opened my bag, looked around in it, put his lime and lemons in it. What do a lime and lemons mean, does anyone know?"

Their jaws dropped. They had put the lime and lemons in my suitcase as a joke during the flight from Cleveland. I hadn't noticed them in the plane or when I looked in my bag before dashing off to practice that afternoon. So it had nothing to do with the maniac.

Nevertheless, I have since changed my phone number and doubled my security precautions.

I don't want to make it sound as though life in Atlanta is all loneliness and scary nights. Sometimes my usually mundane life can be really exciting. I'm invited to receptions, galas, fine meals in the city's best restaurants. I meet charming, very interesting people, stars of film and sports like Mike Gavor, Bruce McNall, Tiger Williams, Ken Dryden, Michael Smith, Rocket Ismail.

It's impressive. These are very well-known people, admired by everyone, but they have remained unaffected. Rubbing shoulders with them, they seem to me to behave like ordinary people, just like you and me. It's a great lesson in life.

Dinner dress, evening gowns, white limousines—it's all very nice, but it's just show. I want to remain little Manon Rhéaume from Lac Beauport. I play the game, it's all part of the job. But all this glamour sometimes embarrasses me, and sometimes it even makes me laugh.

I also get a kick when I find myself sitting among my admirers. Quite often, Quebecers who travel to Atlanta on business come to a Knights game hoping to see me play. But I'm up in the stands with them, watching the game. Once they figure out I'm not in net, they come to find me to say hello and to tell me how proud they are of me. It's embarrassing, but heartwarming, too. And I love speaking with them in French. I must say, I often miss Quebec.

And then there are all the people, young and not-so-young, who ask me for autographs. I never sign during games, because it would never end, and besides, one of the chores I do for Gene Ubriaco involves jotting down statistics. So they wait for me at the Omni Center exit. They scream and pull at my clothing. I get a kick out of it.

It reminds me of when I was young and waited for the Nordiques players to leave the Colisée, my eyes wide like saucers and my mouth open in awe. Happiness was being able to touch one of my heroes!

Unfortunately, I can't make everyone happy. Some fans are disappointed to see me leave after having waited, pen in hand, in vain, hoping I'll sign a hockey card.

Same for the letters I receive—as many as one hundred a day. I would like to answer them all, but it's impossible. I don't have the time. Boxes of letters pile up at the Omni Center, and also in my living and dining rooms. I don't know where to put them any more. It's out of control.

I give priority to people who ask me to sign a card and who make the effort to include a stamped, self-addressed return envelope. That I can handle. As for the others ... I really can't see ever being able to get around to most of them.

People send me all kinds of things to sign: pucks, sweaters, magazines. They send me presents, too: chocolates (my weakness), writing paper, drawings of me in front of the net, photographs of themselves (in case I get lonely at night, I guess). I've even received a portable stereo and some tinned bacon!

People confide in me, tell me their problems. I find that very annoying sometimes. I would like to help them, but I don't know what to say. Some of them have very serious problems and I'm not qualified to give them advice. Their confidence in me is very touching, though, and I'd really like to do something for them.

Others ask me for information about hockey, advice about how to get to be a goalie in the big leagues. Little girls want to know where they can play.

Feminist groups and religious people urge me to reject offers like the one I received from *Playboy*.

People go to a lot of trouble. I have to find a way to answer all of them. I answer as fast as I can. I do a little every night, but I can't see the light at the end of the tunnel.

The day that people started recognizing me on the street was the day I had to come to grips with the fact that I am now a public personality. Obviously, I can't go unnoticed in places frequented by sports fans. People come up to say hello, ask for autographs, offer to buy me a drink. Restaurateurs give me the best seat in the house.

It also depends on what I'm wearing. When I walk around in jeans, T-shirt and ponytail, I am more or less incognito. That's the way I like it.

JEAN BLOUIN,
ATLANTA KNIGHTS TEAMMATE

All the guys on the Knights are very proud of Manon. But it hasn't been easy for her. We were a little skeptical when she first arrived. The guys didn't think she could do much. None of them, including me, believed in her.

When I left Quebec for the Tampa Bay camp, I thought she hadn't had enough time in the juniors to deserve a place at camp. But she surprised me! She surprised everyone.

During the camp, we didn't baby her. We shot the puck to score, to beat her. We shot from every angle, but they didn't get past her. She showed us she could stop the shots. She looked good throughout the training camp. We saw that this was no joke.

Here, in Atlanta, it's the same thing. She practices a lot. Much more than most of the other players. You can see that she's serious and that she wants to improve.

She is one of the guys now. Of course, at the start, there were some comments from the guys in the locker room. But not now. She has won everyone's respect and we're used to her. When she's on the ice, nobody thinks of her as a girl. We don't shoot any easier on her than on Littman, the other goalie. Off the ice, however, maybe we're a bit more careful with our language.

We kid her a lot, a bit like a sister. But we all laugh together. So, if we didn't kid her, she'd feel left out. We know her weak spots and we take advantage of them but she never gets mad. She's good-natured.

Since she does exactly what all the other players do and gets no special treatment, everything's great. Of course, the media are all focused on her. You'd think that might cause some jealousy among some players, but it doesn't seem to be the case. We don't talk about it amongst ourselves. That's it.

The only problem is that she doesn't come drinking often enough with her mates from "the French Connection." She's too busy with all her promotional activities and is always tired in the evening. We just can't get her out. In any case, she's really not a drinker. We discovered that at the initiation.

She really had Daniel Vincelette and me worried the night she had the visit from her nut case. Daniel answered when she telephoned. She was so panicky that he didn't understand much. All he managed to catch was that someone was trying to get into her place, that she was afraid and that she wanted us to come and get her and take her back to our place for at least a night.

I blasted out the door full steam ahead. In my panic, I punched in the wrong code to open the door—the poor guy who answered must have had heart failure, since the tone of my voice announced that he was going to need major surgery after I got hold of him!

We still don't know who tried to force Manon's door, but I swear I will never again put a lime and lemons in a girl's bag. Cross my heart.

11

TO BE CONTINUED ...

When I look back on how far I've come, on everything I've accomplished, I know that I have my parents to thank. They've always supported me and my brothers, both financially and psychologically. They are always supportive, never negative. They make us see the good side of things, even in difficult times.

My parents taught me respect—for others, but mainly for myself.

I'm still the same person, the same little girl from Lac Beauport. I haven't changed my style or my way of speaking. I still call up my friends and visit my beloved cousins and family.

I tend goal because I love it. Now it's my job, and it's fun. I'm living my dream: playing hockey. When I get up in the morning, I'm already in a good mood. I don't have to drag myself out of bed and into the bathroom. I can hardly wait to get on the ice, to learn, to work hard. It's also fun. I can handle the less easy parts, too. They're part of the game. There are good and bad sides to everything in life.

Gene Ubriaco believes in me, and he seems sincere. So does Richard Adler, the Knights' president. Phil Esposito took a chance and he has confidence in me. It's up to me to prove to everyone that there has been no mistake.

I have to silence the skeptics. They have the right to their opinions and I respect them. As long as they respect mine. And as long as they let me try.

Anything that's come my way outside of hockey has come on its own. I never looked for it. I'm just a woman who had a chance of a lifetime and was able to take advantage of it.

For sure, hockey has provided some exciting experiences that I wouldn't have lived doing macramé, but I really don't feel like a star.

What's always been one of my biggest assets, and still is, is that, basically, I'm a realist. Or maybe I should say I'm a realistic dreamer. I love to conjure up visions of things in my head. I dream up scenarios where great things are happening in fantastic locations with wonderful people.

When I really want something to happen, I envision it in my mind. Most of the time it works. I've been doing that ever since I was little, without really ever applying the label "visualization" to the process.

I can see myself in a few years with some lovely kids and a man by my side. I can see the pretty house and the yard filled with flowers. Out back, there's a small indoor rink where we can skate all year round. I imagine myself running my own business in communications or some other field.

But I don't want to talk about my short-term dreams. That could bring bad luck.

For me, this is the chance to live a wonderful experience

and I'm taking full advantage of it. I want to go to the limit of my potential, to see how far the training can take me. If I don't take it seriously, I will never know how much I might have accomplished, and I could never forgive myself for that.

I am ready to make plenty of sacrifices to reach my goals, and no one's going to stop me.